Contents

How to Use Ten-Minute Activities

Keep *Ten-Minute Activities* handy.

- Choose an activity for each subject area—language arts, mathematics, social studies, science, and indoor recess—that is appropriate to the skill level of your students.
- Mark these pages with sticky notes.
- Read through each activity to make sure you understand the steps.
- Gather any materials that must be prepared in advance, label them with the activity name and page number, and set them aside.
- After you use an activity, immediately choose and prepare another in that subject area so that you always have five activities ready to go.

Although these short activities do not require teaching a lesson to execute, it is always best to plan ahead just as you would for a lesson in any subject.

Many of the activities require no materials; others require no more than paper and pencils. Activities with more materials listed will probably require some advance preparation.

For activities done in small groups, you can save time if groups are designated in advance. If you seat your students in clusters of desks or tables, you may, of course, use seating as the group designator. Or you may prepare and post a chart of partners and groups. Be sure to include the location where each group is to meet. When the need for a 10-minute activity arises, you need only say, "Gather with your group."

My Pet Porcupine

by Eve Timm

▶ **Materials:** none

▶ **Here's How!**

1. This game is based on the jump rope rhyme "A my name is Annie." Have each student choose an animal, a name, and a food that all begin with the same letter.

2. Then have the students complete the following sentence frame with their words.

   My pet _____'s name is _____ and it eats _____.

3. Try keeping the same animal, changing the name and food if desired.

4. For a challenge, create the rhymes alphabetically!

My pet <u>porcupine</u>'s name is <u>Pete</u> and it eats <u>potatoes</u>.

The Alliteration Game

by Eve Timm

▶ **Materials:** none

▶ **Here's How!**

Here's an activity that can be done as a follow-up to reading Laura Numeroff's book *If You Give a Moose a Muffin.*

1. Draw students' attention to the pattern of the beginning sounds of *moose* and *muffin*.

2. Ask each student to think of an animal and a food that begin with the same letter.

3. Then have the student complete the repeated pattern, "I gave a _____ a _____."

4. Challenge your students to think of different animals and foods each time.

▶ **Variation**

Play a similar game, substituting a student's name for the animal name.

I gave a <u>dog</u> a <u>doughnut</u>.

I'm Going To . . .
by Eve Timm

▶ **Materials:** none

▶ **Here's How!**

1. Begin this game by choosing a location anywhere in the world that you might like to travel to.

2. Choose any object to take with you on your trip that begins with the same letter. For example, "I'm going to Antarctica and I'm taking an anteater!"

3. Have each student, in turn, name a place and an object in the same manner.

4. Continue play until all students have had the chance to participate.

▶ **Variation**

Play the same game in alphabetical order, with the first student choosing a country and an object beginning with the letter *a*. The second student uses the letter *b*, and so on.

I'm going to Kenya and I'm taking a kelly green jacket.

Sounds Bingo
by Susan Kunze

▶ **Materials:** chalkboard, chalk, student copies of a blank Bingo grid, pencil or construction-paper squares

▶ **Here's How!**

B	I	N	G	O
ch	L	z	a	th
fr	s	p	r	n
gl	qu	FREE	j	gr
sh	b	e	wh	g
bl	t	c	m	h

1. List on the chalkboard and sound out together 24 sounds your students should know. These may be single sounds, blends, digraphs, or word families. Students write the letters that spell those sounds in the squares on their Bingo board in any order they like.

2. Choose a sound from the list. One way to do this is to write the sounds on small slips of paper and place them in a container to randomly select one at a time. A simpler way to do this is to jot the list on a piece of paper and place a mark next to it so it won't be duplicated.

3. Say the sound carefully and then repeat it. Students find the corresponding letter(s) on their grids and then cross out or cover them.

4. Students play this like Bingo, looking for five sounds in a row, horizontally, vertically, or diagonally. The first student with five in a row wins the game.

▶ **Variations**

- To simplify this game, use the same sound more than once in the original list. Students cross out or cover only one sound at a time.

- For younger students, this game may be played using the names of the letters instead of the sounds.

- For quicker or simpler games, use 16-square Bingo grids.

Next in Line

by Eve Timm

▶ **Materials:** none

▶ **Here's How!**

1. Begin this activity by selecting a word. Any word will work. You may want to choose one that relates to your curriculum.

2. Ask the students to listen for the last sound they hear in the word.

3. Ask a student to think of another word that begins with the ending sound of the previous word.

4. Continue in this manner, allowing different students to provide new words.

▶ **Variations**

• As your students become familiar with this game, challenge them to think of words in a category. For example:

  food—banana, avocado, orange

• Play the same game, but each time a word is offered, require the student to spell it.

Finish the Word

by Doug and Sharman Wurst

▶ **Materials:** chalkboard, chalk

▶ **Here's How!**

1. Write a blend or digraph on the chalkboard.

2. Instruct the students to tell as many words as possible that begin with those letters.

   Other suggested blends or digraphs include *gr, bl, pr, qu, th, sn, ch,* and *fr.*

▶ **Variation**

Have students use dictionaries to find words with different blends and digraphs.

wh

what   whale
where   which
when   wheel
why   whatever

Grab that blue quilt, I'm freezing!

Word Family Scramble
by Susan Kunze

▶ **Materials:** chart paper, marker, paper, pencils

▶ **Here's How!**

1. Write a word family on the chart. (See the examples at right.)

2. Have students work in pairs or small groups for 3 to 5 minutes to write as many words as possible using that word family. Find the group with the most words and list those words on the chart.

3. Check with the class to see if any other groups have different examples to add.

4. If time permits, have students alphabetize their lists.

ock

clock	cockle
mock	frock
block	dock
flock	lock

High-Frequency Word Families

ack	ail	ain	ake	all	ight	ill	in	ine	ing	ink	ip	it
ame	an	ank	ap	ash	ell	est	ice	ick	ide	ock	oke	
at	ate	aw	ay	eat	op	ore	ot	uck	ug	ump	unk	

I've Been to Many Places!

by Eve Timm

▶ **Materials:** none

▶ **Here's How!**

1. Have the students sit in a circle and choose a starting person.

2. The class says, in unison, "I have been to many places."

3. Then the first student chosen says, "I have been to _____," filling in the blank with a location.

4. The class repeats the sentence and moves around the circle with each new student adding a new place.

5. Ask the students not to repeat any location that has already been mentioned.

▶ **Variation**

For a challenge, try this game by naming locations in alphabetical order!

Book Sale

by Doug and Sharman Wurst

▶ **Materials:** none

▶ **Here's How!**

1. Ask each student to think of a favorite book that he or she has recently read.

2. Have students take turns acting as salespeople, trying to sell their favorite books.

Sales pitches could include:
how wonderful the characters were
why the book was exciting
a display of the best illustrations
who might enjoy reading the book

You've just got to read
Where the Wild Things Are!
The kid has such a great time doing
stuff he doesn't usually get to do.
I kept wondering if he'd get
to come home, though. Here's my
favorite picture...

Speak Right Up!

by Jennifer Norris

▶ **Materials:** a microphone (or an object representing a microphone)

▶ **Here's How!**

1. Have the students sit at desks or tables.

2. Hold the "microphone" and ask a question such as, "What did you do in school today?"

3. Hold the microphone in front of one student at a time as answers are reported.

▶ **Variations**

- Interview students about specific information in a story or unit studied.

- Have each student assume the role of a character in a story and respond to the question as that character.

Today in school I hit a home run!

Skittish

by Laurie Williams

▶ **Materials:** labeled papers (see below)

▶ **Here's How!**

1. In advance, label papers identically with the name of a person, a place, and a thing. (See examples below.)

2. Divide students into groups of four or five.

3. Give each group one of the labeled papers.

4. Each group must make up a skit to perform that contains all three subjects. For example: Each group is given a piece of paper with the words: Big Bird (person), zoo (place), and popcorn (thing). They might make up a skit about Big Bird going to the zoo and buying popcorn, or about someone going to see Big Bird at the zoo and feeding him popcorn.

Skit Prompts
1. explorer, jungle, river
2. astronaut, Mars, alien
3. child, playground, ball game
4. swimmer, ocean, shark
5. shopper, toy store, electronic game

I'm Going on a Picnic!
by Eve Timm

▶ **Materials:** none

▶ **Here's How!**

1. Secretly choose a category. (See the box below for suggestions.)

2. Say, "I'm going on a picnic and I'm taking a _____." (Fill in the blank with something from your category.) For example:

   I'm going on a picnic and I'm taking a poodle.

3. Continue repeating the pattern with a new clue each time. For example:

   I'm going on a picnic and I'm taking a poodle and a Dalmatian.

   I'm going on a picnic and I'm taking a poodle, a Dalmatian, and a husky.

4. Students raise their hands when they think they know the category. When called on, the student repeats the entire sentence and adds a new item to take along. For example:

   I'm going on a picnic and I'm taking a poodle, a Dalmatian, a husky, and a golden retriever.

5. If the student is correct, say, "Yes, you can go on the picnic with me!" If incorrect, say, "Sorry, try again."

African animals—an elephant, a gorilla, a lion,
     a giraffe, etc.
fruits—a watermelon, a guava, a strawberry,
     a kiwi, etc.
red things—red lipstick, a stop sign, a delicious
     apple, etc.
alphabetical order—an airplane, a banana,
     a cat, etc.

Word Links

by Doug and Sharman Wurst

▶ **Materials:** none

▶ **Here's How!**

1. Announce a category to the class, such as animals, plants, cities, states, colors, or numbers. Say a word that would fit into that category.

2. Students raise their hands to say other words in that category.

3. Announce a new category when no more words are offered.

4. Have one student keep a tally of the number of words for each category. The class should try to beat the highest score each time.

▶ **Variation**

Have students say words that begin with the same letter. For example: If the category is colors that start with "b," answers might include blue, brown, black, and so on.

Guess the Author!

by Eve Timm

▶ **Materials:** none

▶ **Here's How!**

1. Prepare a list of familiar children's authors and the books they have written.

2. Tell the class that you are going to play "Guess the Author."

3. Provide students with a clue or a book title. Allow time for responses.

4. Continue to provide clues until the author is successfully identified.

▶ **Variation**

Try the same activity using illustrators of children's books!

Who Uses It?

by Eve Timm

▶ **Materials:** none

▶ **Here's How!**

1. Say the name of a tool and have the class brainstorm a person or people who could use it. For example, a hammer could be used by a carpenter, a handyman, or even by a parent.

2. Draw the students' attention to the fact that many of the same tools are used in different jobs.

3. Brainstorm a new use for one of these common tools:

hammer	spoon	computer
calculator	eraser	toothbrush
pencil	comb	scissors
pliers	saw	stethoscope

▶ **Variation**

Write the name of an occupation on the chalkboard. Have each student list all of the tools a person might use to perform that job. Invite students to share and compare their lists.

What Can You Do with It?

by Jennifer Norris

▶ **Materials:** chalkboard, chalk

▶ **Here's How!**

1. Ask the students, "What can you do with an apple?"

2. Record their responses on the chalkboard.

>   Examples: ball, snack, juggle, decoration, paperweight, wash it, cut it up, dip it in caramel

3. Continue in the same manner with other objects. See the box below for suggestions.

baby bottle	book	belt	shoe	scissors
flowerpot	lunch box	waffle iron	tree	

▶ **Variation**

Divide the class into small groups and see which group comes up with the most responses.

Finish It Your Way

by Jennifer Norris

▶ **Materials:** paper, pencils

▶ **Here's How!**

1. Recite a familiar nursery rhyme and ask a question about what could happen next.

   Little Miss Muffet sat on a tuffet,
   Eating her curds and whey;
   Along came a spider who sat down beside her,
   And frightened Miss Muffet away.

   Where did Miss Muffet go?

2. Have students write for 3 minutes in response to the question.

3. Allow them to share their responses.

▶ **Variation**

Read a portion of a literature story and have students write about what could happen next.

The Same Game

by Laurie Williams

▶ **Materials:** none

▶ **Here's How!**

1. Choose three students who have something in common (long hair, blue jeans, braces, missing teeth, or glasses) to stand in the front of the room.

2. Ask the remaining students in the class to guess what all three students have in common by asking only questions requiring "yes" or "no" answers.

3. The student who correctly guesses chooses three more students with a common trait and answers "yes" and "no" to the questions posed.

   The dialogue may be as follows:

Student #1:	Does the similarity have to do with clothing?
Teacher:	Yes.
Student #2:	Is the similarity something on their backs?
Teacher:	No.
Student #3:	Is the similarity above the waist?
Teacher:	No.
Student #4:	Is the similarity that they all have on shoes?
Teacher:	No.
Student #5:	Is it that they all have at least one shoe untied?
Teacher:	Yes! Now you get to choose three students.

Secret Message

by Susan Kunze

▶ **Materials:** chalkboard, chalk, paper, pencils

▶ **Here's How!**

1. Write the alphabet across the chalkboard. Write the numbers (sequentially) 1 through 26 below each letter to make a code.

2. Write a short sentence using the number code. For example:

9	12 9 11 5	9 3 5	3 18 5 1 13
I	**like**	**ice**	**cream.**

13 25	13 15 13	2 1 11 5 4	3 15 15 11 9 5 19
My	**mom**	**baked**	**cookies.**

3. Students use the number code to decode the message.

▶ **Variation**

Students use the number code to write their own sentences for partners to decode.

Guess the Book!

by Eve Timm

▶ **Materials:** none

▶ **Here's How!**

1. Choose a book that you have recently used in your class. The goal is to guess the book title while reviewing genre and story aspects.

2. Give clues related to the book's genre and story structure. Begin with clues that don't give the book title away instantly. For example:

    It is a fictional story.
    The setting is . . .
    One of the characters is . . .
    One event in the plot is . . .

▶ **Variation**

Print the title of each book shared in class on a separate index card. A student chooses a card and provides clues to the book title for the class to guess.

It is a nonfiction book. The content area is *math*. Something new we learned was . . .

A Long Sentence

by Jennifer Norris

▶ **Materials:** chalkboard, chalk, paper, pencils

▶ **Here's How!**

1. Write a three-word phrase or sentence on the chalkboard.

2. Ask the students to add adjectives and phrases to make the sentence longer.

   This morning the rickety old school bus stopped in front of the school just before the bell rang.

3. Count the words in the sentence.

4. Write another sentence, adding even more words.

▶ **Variation**

Encourage the addition of conjunctions and verbs.

A bus stopped.

Describe a Snack
by Doug and Sharman Wurst

▶ **Materials:** graham crackers, paper, pencils

▶ **Here's How!**

1. Give each student a graham cracker.

2. Have them describe the color, smell, appearance, texture, and taste of the snack.

3. Read the example found in the box to the students.

> The graham cracker has the color of a honey bear, the smell of cinnamon, the shape of an envelope, the crispy crunch of a breakfast cereal, and a tangy, sweet taste.

▶ **Variation**

Repeat this activity using different kinds of snacks. Save the descriptions and then play a game where the description is read and students guess the identity of the snack.

Acrostic Poem

by Doug and Sharman Wurst

▶ **Materials:** paper, pencils

▶ **Here's How!**

1. Have students write acrostic poems using their first names.

2. Each student writes his or her name, vertically, and then uses each letter as the first letter of a self-descriptive word or phrase. (See the example below.)

3. Encourage the use of words of affirmation.

▶ **Variation**

Write an acrostic poem as a whole class project.

Pretty eyes
Always polite
Takes turns
Team player
Young hearted

Add an Adjective!
by Eve Timm

▶**Materials:** none

▶**Here's How!**

1. This is a progressive game in which each student adds an adjective to a noun that you announce to the class.

2. As each student adds a new adjective, he or she repeats all of the previous ones added. For example:

> The alligator
> The big alligator
> The big, hungry alligator
> The big, hungry, scaly alligator
> The big, hungry, scaly, purple alligator

3. Play continues until the sequence is broken. Resume play by providing a new noun.

Word Hunt

by Doug and Sharman Wurst

▶ **Materials:** chalkboard, chalk, paper, pencils

▶ **Here's How!**

1. Give your students 2 minutes to write as many adjectives (describing words) as possible.

2. Select five students at a time to write their one or two best words on the chalkboard.

3. Erase duplicate words and correct misspellings.

4. Groups of students continue to write their words on the board.

5. Continue in this manner until all students have written their words.

6. Use the words to create sentences as a class.

▶ **Variation**

Instead of using adjectives, have students brainstorm verbs, adverbs, or other parts of speech.

huge   funny

prickly   crooked

fuzzy   spotted

In Other Words

by Jennifer Norris

▶ **Materials:** chart paper, marking pens

▶ **Here's How!**

1. Divide students into small groups. Assign each group a common verb.

2. Have each group brainstorm other words that could be used in place of the common verb.

3. Have each group record its words on the chart paper.

4. Compile a class list.

▶ **Variations**

* Ask students to give the past tense of the verb.

* Write action verbs on index cards. Have students draw pictures representing the verbs.

* Choose groups of words, such as nouns related to a unit of study or words showing spatial relationships.

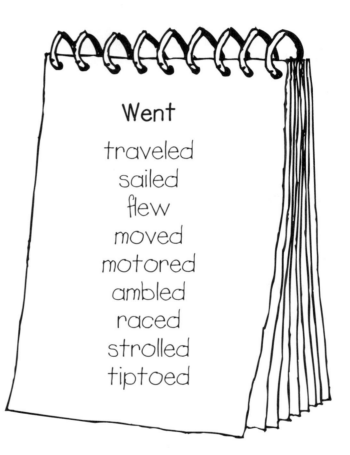

Went
traveled
sailed
flew
moved
motored
ambled
raced
strolled
tiptoed

Desk Aerobics

by Laurie Williams

▶ **Materials:** chalkboard, chalk

▶ **Here's How!**

1. On the chalkboard, write the information at right.

2. Read a sentence and ask the students to decide if the verb tense is past, present, or future. The students indicate their choices by standing behind, beside, or in front of their desks.

3. Read the sentences from the box below and ask students to identify the verbs and explain why they are positioned where they are around their desks.

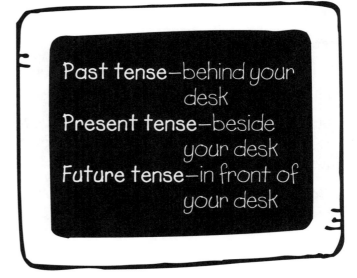

Past tense—behind your desk
Present tense—beside your desk
Future tense—in front of your desk

Alan **drove** his car to the gas station.
Past tense (behind the desk)

The flag **will be lowered** before it gets dark.
Future tense (in front of the desk)

Dad and his brother **are shaking** hands.
Present tense (beside the desk)

His sister **knows** how to count to twenty in three languages.
Present tense (beside the desk)

I **read** the directions on the back of the box.
Past tense (behind the desk)

Erin and Abigail **will fly** to Minnesota on Thursday.
Future tense (in front of the desk)

What Have You Seen?

by Eve Timm

▶ **Materials:** none

▶ **Here's How!**

1. This game helps students use the irregular verb *seen* correctly. Begin by having the students sit in a circle.

2. Say, "I have seen a _____. What have you seen?" (Add anything you want in the blank.) For example, you might say, "I have seen a marvelous moose. What have you seen?"

3. Go around the circle having each student, in turn, answer the question in the same manner. Each time the student ends his or her turn by saying, "What have you seen?"

4. Play for as long as time allows.

My Friend and I
by Eve Timm

▶ **Materials:** none

▶ **Here's How!**

This activity provides great practice in the correct use of *I*.

1. Ask each student to think of a friend's name.

2. The student then chooses an activity that he or she and the friend can do together.

3. Model the correct way to form a sentence in this way by saying a sentence such as, "Jake and I like to ride bikes" or "Susie and I walked to the park." Emphasize the use of the word *I* rather than *me*.

4. Go around the room asking each student to provide a correct sentence. To improve creative thinking and listening skills, encourage students not to repeat names or activities that have already been used.

Max and I are ready for supper!

Ten-Minute Activities for Grades 1–3 • EMC 784

Interesting Idioms
by Susan Kunze

▶ **Materials:** chalkboard, chalk

▶ **Here's How!**

1. List several idioms on the chalkboard. (See below for ideas.)

2. Discuss the literal and interpretive meanings of each.

3. Invite students to use the idioms in sentences or even act them out.

Idioms

being on top of the world	got up on the wrong side of the bed
bit off more than you could chew	bent over backward
jumped down my throat	feel like a million dollars
having a broken heart	in the same boat
keep an eye out	to get cold feet
feeling under the weather	a piece of cake
having a green thumb	get on the ball
being in a pickle	hitting the roof
hitting the sack	zip your lip

Rhyme Time

by Jennifer Norris

▶ **Materials:** chart paper, marker

▶ **Here's How!**

1. Announce a simple word such as *cat, mouse,* or *fish.*

2. Ask your students to name all the words they can think of that rhyme with it.

3. As a class, create a sentence using as many of the rhyming words as possible.

▶ **Variation**

Divide the class into small groups to see which of the groups can think of the most rhyming words. Have the groups compare their sentences.

fish
dish
wish
selfish
Trish

My friend Trish made a selfish wish for a dish with a fish in it.

Yankee Doodle Follies

by Doug and Sharman Wurst

▶ **Materials:** none

▶ **Here's How!**

1. Teach the song "Yankee Doodle."

    Yankee Doodle went to town, riding on a pony
    Stuck a feather in his hat, and called it macaroni
    Yankee Doodle keep it up, Yankee Doodle dandy
    Mind the music and the step and keep the girls handy.

2. Students suggest new rhyming words to replace *pony* and *macaroni*. The sillier the new words the better. For example:

    kitty—oh so pretty
    giraffe—a good laugh
    poodle—a wet noodle
    panda—Miss Amanda
    turtle—jump a hurdle

3. Sing the song using the new rhyming words.

▶ **Variation**

For older students, require that the first word have two syllables and the second word have four syllables.

Descriptive Synonyms

by Eve Timm

▶ **Materials:** chart paper, markers

▶ **Here's How!**

1. Prepare a list of common words such as *nice, good, happy, sad,* and *big.*

2. Explain to the students that synonyms are words that mean the same or almost the same thing.

3. Divide the students into small groups and assign a common word to each group. Ask the students to think of descriptive synonyms that could be used in place of the common word.

4. Provide each group with marking pens and chart paper for recording brainstormed words.

5. Post each list of synonyms and allow time for the class to add to each list. Encourage students to use the synonyms in their writing in place of common words.

Nice

pleasant
pleasing
lovely
friendly
kind
polite
fine

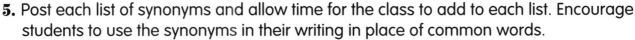

Good—excellent, superior, first-rate, fine, enjoyable, top-notch, well-behaved, delicious, tasty, scrumptious
Happy—thrilled, contented, pleased, glad, joyful, cheerful
Sad—woeful, tearful, mournful, miserable, cheerless, gloomy
Big—enormous, tremendous, gigantic, gargantuan, colossal

You Write the Ending

by Doug and Sharman Wurst

▶ **Materials:** chalkboard, chalk, paper, pencils

▶ **Here's How!**

1. On the chalkboard, write one of the sentence starters found in the box below.

2. Have students finish writing the sentence in as humorous a way as possible.

3. Share the silly sentences.

4. Continue with new sentence starters as time allows.

The first time I flew in a plane, the plane...

When I took my hamster out of the cage, it...
When I jumped out of a swing...
As I was holding my pet snake...
During an experiment, I poured two chemicals together and...
I had a dream last night about a monster that...
When I was digging in the dirt, I found...
As I was looking through my telescope, I saw...

Journal Jive

by Doug and Sharman Wurst

▶ **Materials:** journal or paper, pencils

▶ **Here's How!**

Have students write about one of the following questions or sentence starters:

If you had a thousand dollars to give away, who would you give it to and why?

If you could go anywhere in the world, where would you go and why?

Tell about the school subject you are best in.

Tell about the school subject you would like to improve in.

What makes a good friend?

If you could spend the day with anyone, who would it be? What would you do?

So far today, I have learned…

I want to learn about _____ because…

Thank You, Thank You

by Jennifer Norris

▶ **Materials:** chart paper, marking pens, length of ribbon

▶ **Here's How!**

1. Choose a school support person, such as the custodian, the cook, or the secretary.

2. Write a class note thanking the person for his or her help at school, by having students dictate as you write their thoughts on chart paper.

3. Each student signs the thank you note.

4. Roll up the message and tie it with a ribbon. Deliver the note to the designated person.

▶ **Variation**

Have students write their own notes to selected people who offer assistance at school.

Making a Quick Thank-You Card

by Doug and Sharman Wurst

▶ **Materials:** an index card for each student, a large sheet of construction paper

▶ **Here's How!**

The guest speaker just left and it's 10 minutes before recess. Make this quick thank-you card to show your appreciation.

1. Fold a large sheet of construction paper in half horizontally to make a card.

2. Write on the front of the card "Thank you from Us All."

3. Give each student an index card to write a personal note of thanks.

4. Glue the index cards inside the folded construction paper to make a class card.

Scrambled Eggs
by Eve Timm

▶ **Materials:** none

▶ **Here's How!**

1. Have the students line up in a particular sequence, such as:

   • tallest to shortest
   • alphabetically by first names
   • alphabetically by last names
   • number of letters in names

2. Then say, "Scrambled eggs!" The students move around the classroom. (Remind students that eggs can't talk!)

3. When they are thoroughly scrambled say, "Sequence," and see how fast they can line up in the right order.

If you practice this throughout the year, your students will line up quickly for class pictures, health screenings, etc.

Alphabet Chains

by Susan Kunze

▶ **Materials:** chalkboard, chalk, 1" x 6" (2.5 x 15 cm) strips of paper, glue

▶ **Here's How!**

1. On the chalkboard, list several spelling or vocabulary words you want your students to alphabetize. Younger students should use words that start with different letters and alphabetize to the first letter only. Older students may use words that can be alphabetized to the second, third, or fourth letter.

2. A student writes each of the words in the center of a different strip of paper, and then lays them in alphabetical order. Partners check each other's work.

3. Students glue the first strip end-to-end to make a circle and then glue each consecutive strip onto the last to make an alphabetical chain.

▶ **Variation**

Make chains of compound words by writing the first word of the compound on the first strip. Students then chain on words that can make compounds with that word. Examples:

air—plane, port, tight
back—pack, yard, bone, ache, ground
book—mark, store, seller
home—work, made, sick
in—door, field, side, to
snow—man, ball, flake, plow, storm
some—place, day, time, where, thing
water—color, fall, melon, front

Alphabetizing Line-Up

by Susan Kunze

▶ **Materials:** index cards

▶ **Here's How!**

1. Each child writes his or her name on an index card.

2. The students line up in alphabetical order, looking at each other's cards to determine where they belong in line. (Younger students line up by first letters only, grouping students whose names start with the same letters. Older students may alphabetize to the second, third, or fourth letters.)

3. Students then say their names, beginning with the first letter of the alphabet and proceeding to the end. Encourage students to determine if each name is in alphabetical order and then sequence themselves appropriately.

▶ **Variations**

Have students line up according to:

- last names
- favorite characters from a variety of stories
- names of pets, siblings, or other relatives
- favorite sports, animals, toys, or games

How Many Syllables?

by Eve Timm

▶ **Materials:** none

▶ **Here's How!**

1. Prepare a list of one-, two-, and three-syllable words or grab a textbook.

2. Read a word and then ask students to indicate the number of syllables by holding up the corresponding number of fingers.

3. After students have the idea of the activity, allow individuals to give a word. The rest of the class counts the syllables and holds up the correct number of fingers.

▶ **Variation**

Say a different student's name each time and ask the students to identify the number of syllables.

Contraction Action

by Laurie Williams

▶**Materials:** index cards (see below), marking pens

▶**Here's How!**

1. In advance, prepare a set of index cards, labeled with the following words, for each group of three or four students.

do	am	is	has
not	had	are	must
will	can	did	we
I	would	should	have

2. Distribute a set of cards to each group.

3. The students in the groups match cards that can create contractions. For example: *did* + *not* = *didn't.* Explain that some words can be used in more than one way. For example, *is* can be used in the contractions *isn't* and *she's.*

▶**Variation**

Have students work in small groups to make different contractions.

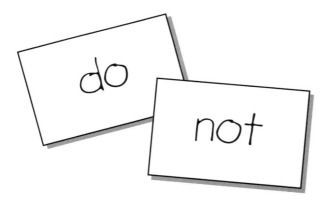

Alphabet Soup
by Laurie Williams

▶ **Materials:** chalkboard, chalk, paper, pencils

▶ **Here's How!**

1. On the chalkboard, write only the letters in the first, middle, or final third of the alphabet:

   A B C D E F G H   I J K L M N O P Q   R S T U V W X Y Z

2. Give students several minutes to write as many words as they can using only those letters.

3. Write the words students made on the chalkboard.

4. Repeat the activity using the other parts of the alphabet as time allows.

▶ **Variation**

Create words in which every letter is in alphabetical order. For example:

   best   adopt   him   mop   city

The Long Vowel Game

by Eve Timm

▶ **Materials:** chalkboard, chalk, or chart paper, marker, index cards

▶ **Here's How!**

1. Choose a long vowel to use for this game.

2. Begin by saying, "The word *day* has a long *a* sound. Can you think of another word that has the same *a* sound as in *day*?" As a class, brainstorm a list of long *a* words and write them on the chalkboard or chart paper.

day   hay   say
angel   ape   cape
play   may   lay

3. Look for patterns in the words, such as words ending in silent *e* or *ay*.

4. Sort the words by patterns such as *make, take,* and *bake* or *day, way,* and *play.*

5. Once you have the words organized by word families, write each one on an index card that can then be placed in a learning center for students to mix up and reorganize.

6. Challenge your students to add to the list whenever they can.

▶ **Variation**

Make a list of words that do not follow phonetic rules. For example, the word *neighbor* isn't spelled with an *a*, but has the long *a* sound being featured. Post these words and add to them.

Words, Words, Words!

by Eve Timm

▶ **Materials:** chalkboard, chalk, paper, pencils

▶ **Here's How!**

1. Write four consonants and two vowels on the chalkboard.

2. Ask the class to think of as many words as they can using the letters you have written.

3. To keep everyone engaged, have the students write their ideas on paper or in writing journals.

4. Have students write their words on the board.

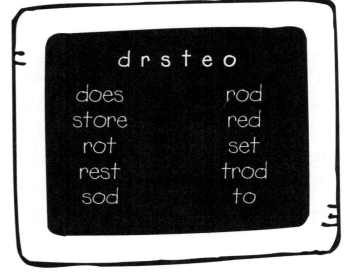

5. A student who thinks of the same word as one on the chalkboard should place a checkmark beside it on his or her paper.

6. Continue to add a new consonant or vowel to see how long your class list will grow!

▶ **Variation**

Experiment with different vowels and consonants each time you try this activity.

Sign It!

by Eve Timm

▶ **Materials:** American Sign Language alphabet (see inside back cover), transparency, overhead projector

▶ **Here's How!**

1. Duplicate the American Sign Language alphabet found on the inside back cover onto a transparency and display it for the class.

2. Divide your students into small groups and assign each group one of your weekly spelling words.

3. Each group determines how to sign the word and then signs it to the class.

4. Other students try to determine which word is being signed.

5. Continue in this manner, spelling each of the weekly words.

Word Find

by Doug and Sharman Wurst

▶ **Materials:** chalkboard, chalk, or chart paper, marker, paper, pencils (optional)

▶ **Here's How!**

1. Write on the chalkboard or chart nine letters in three rows of three. There must be one vowel in each horizontal row. (See the example at right.)

2. Explain the rules:

   • Connect letters to form words.

   • You may connect letters up, down, or across.

   • The letters may be used again for a new word.

   • A letter may be used only once in each word.

3. As each word is found, call on a student to touch the letters and spell the word. Keep a list of the words on the chalkboard. You may want students to record the words on their own.

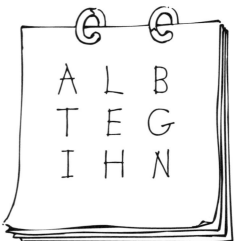

Words Made from the Example
a at it beg bet ten net hit tea hi get leg let the late neat teal heal heat then beat

▶ **Variation**

Use a 16-letter grid with four letters in four rows.

Morphing Spelling

by Doug and Sharman Wurst

▶ **Materials:** chalkboard, chalk

▶ **Here's How!**

1. Write *milk* on the chalkboard.

2. Tell students, "We are to change a letter in this word to make a new word." Show students that by changing the *m* to an *s,* the word *silk* is formed. Then by changing the *k* to an *l,* the word *sill* is formed. Continue with the demonstration, verbalizing each change.

3. After the demonstration, write another word on the board such as *hand*. Have a student change a letter of the word and write the new word below it.

4. Select another student to change a letter of the new word to create another. For example:

    hand   ha**r**d   **c**ard   c**o**rd   col**d**

5. Play continues in this manner, allowing all students to participate.

More Examples

tail	car
tall	far
mall	fir
malt	fit
melt	mit

Word Scramble

by Doug and Sharman Wurst

▶ **Materials:** chart paper, marker, pencils

▶ **Here's How!**

1. Draw a circle on the chart.

2. Write a scrambled spelling word in the circle.

3. Have students unscramble the letters and write the word on their papers. (See the examples below.)

o d	e m
r w	c o
word	come

Scrabbling Words

by Susan Kunze

▶ **Materials:** chalkboard, chalk, paper, pencils

▶ **Here's How!**

1. Write current spelling or vocabulary words on the chalkboard.

2. Challenge students to connect three or more words by crossing them as in the game Scrabble®. For example:

   words—before, morning, large, horse
   warning, start, partner

Spelling Baseball

by Jennifer Norris

▶ **Materials:** three chairs

▶ **Here's How!**

1. Designate three chairs as bases and arrange them like a baseball diamond.

2. Say or "pitch" a spelling word to a "batter."

3. The batter spells the word. If the word is spelled correctly, the batter sits in the first-base chair and becomes a "runner." If the word is spelled incorrectly, the batter is out.

4. Additional batters advance runners around the bases. A run is scored when a player advances after sitting on "third base."

5. Add interest to this game by assigning extra minutes at recess or another enticing reward for each run scored.

▶ **Variation**

Set a class goal. For example, try to score more runs than were scored the previous time the game was played.

Password

by Eve Timm

▶ **Materials:** index cards

▶ **Here's How**

1. Secretly show a student one of your weekly spelling words written on an index card.

2. The student provides clues to the class and they try to guess the word. Clues may include the number of letters, synonyms, ending or beginning sounds, or vowel patterns.

This word has five letters.
It begins with a blend.
It rhymes with *brass*.
Many people have this in their yards.

Answer: grass

First-Letter Shapes
by Susan Kunze

▶ **Materials:** chalkboard, chalk, paper, pencils

▶ **Here's How!**

1. Write spelling or vocabulary words on the chalkboard.

2. Have students write each word several times to form the shape of the first letter of that word.

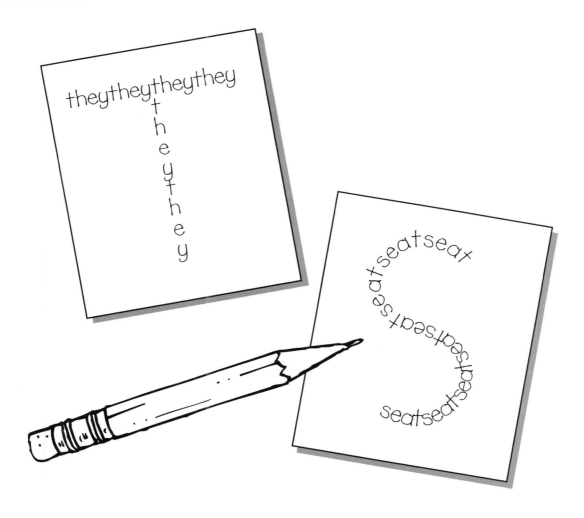

The Goose Spot Game!

by Eve Timm

▶ **Materials:** chalkboard, chalk, or chart paper, marking pens

▶ **Here's How!**

This game can be quite challenging. You might need to write the words on the chalkboard so the class can look for patterns.

1. Choose two related words. One **must** be spelled with **double letters**, and the **other must not**. Current spelling words work best, or use the names of objects around the room.

2. Tell students that the object of the game is to determine what makes something a "goose spot."

3. Begin by saying, "A b<u>oo</u>k is a g<u>oo</u>se spot, but paper is not."

4. Continue to give clues. Here are some suggestions:

   The fl<u>oo</u>r is a goose spot, but the ceiling is not.
   A b<u>oo</u>t is a goose spot, but a shoe is not.
   Gr<u>ee</u>n is a goose spot, but red is not.
   Spe<u>ll</u>ing is a goose spot, but reading is not.
   St<u>oo</u>l is a goose spot, but chair is not.
   The scr<u>ee</u>n on the computer is a goose spot, but the keyboard is not.
   A mi<u>tt</u>en is a goose spot, but a glove is not.
   A b<u>oo</u>k is a goose spot, but a magazine is not.

5. When a student thinks he or she has discovered the pattern, the student tries to give a new clue instead of simply telling the answer *(The goose spot has double letters in it!)*. If this is too challenging, let the student whisper the answer to you.

6. Play as long as time and clues allow. It would be fun to give a goose spot (a sticker) to each student who correctly guesses the answer.

▶ **Variation**

Play the game using a spelling pattern on the spelling list being studied that week. This will get students to look more carefully at their spelling words.

The Silent "E" Game

by Eve Timm

▶ **Materials:** chart paper, marking pens

▶ **Here's How!**

1. In advance, write CVC (consonant/vowel/consonant) words on a chart. (See the examples at right.)

can	man	kit
nap	van	hat
sit	mop	pan
rod	tub	mat
grip		

2. Read the CVC words with the class. Talk about the spelling pattern in each word (consonant, vowel, consonant). For each word ask, "What vowel sound do you hear? Is that a short or long vowel sound?"

3. Then ask students, "Can you make new words by adding the same letter to the end of each short vowel word?" Guide students until someone responds, "the letter *e.*"

4. Rewrite each word, adding the silent *e.* Ask students to read the new word. For each word ask, "What vowel sound do you hear? Is that a short or long vowel sound?"

can cane	man mane	kit kite
nap nape	van vane	hat hate
sit site	mop mope	pan pane
rod rode	tub tube	mat mate
grip gripe		

5. Help students state the silent *e* rule—*When a silent e is added to the end of a CVC word, the vowel sound changes from short to long.*

Outline Your Name

by Susan Kunze

▶ **Materials:** strips of graph paper, crayons

▶ **Here's How!**

1. Have each student write his or her name on graph paper. Short letters such as *a, c, e, o,* and *m* use one box. Use two boxes for tall letters, such as *b, f,* and *h.*

2. The students then outline their names by tracing the outside edges of the boxes.

3. Then have the students walk around the room comparing names, looking for someone else whose name has the same shape.

▶ **Variations**

Try this with other words, such as:

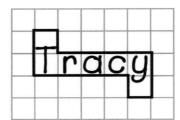

• vocabulary words

• words selected from a story

• words taken from students' writing

• favorite toys, games, and foods

Vowel/Consonant Colors

by Susan Kunze

▶ **Materials:** chalkboard, chalk, crayons (two colors), paper

▶ **Here's How!**

1. Write spelling or vocabulary words on the chalkboard.

2. Have students copy each word on paper using crayons. One color should be used to write the vowels and the other color to write the consonants.

3. Encourage students to talk about the vowel patterns they see in the words.

4. If time permits, list the words on the board according to their vowel patterns. For example, list and contrast words that follow the consonant/vowel/consonant/silent *e* pattern or the consonant/vowel/consonant pattern.

CVC	CVCE
cap	bake
tab	cane
mat	bike

59

Subject Area Word Walls

by Eve Timm

▶ **Materials:** chart paper, marking pen, index cards

▶ **Here's How!**

Whenever you have some extra time in any subject period—social studies, science, math, health, music, art—start or add to a word wall chart for that subject.

1. Fold the bottom piece of chart paper up about 4" (10 cm) and staple to make a pocket. Write the subject area on the pocket.

2. With your students, brainstorm words from the subject area and write them on the chart.

3. Place index cards in the pocket.

4. Staple the chart to a designated "word wall."

5. Invite students to write additional words on index cards and place them in the pocket when they have spare time.

6. Return to the chart at another time, evaluate any student responses on the index cards, and add appropriate words to the chart.

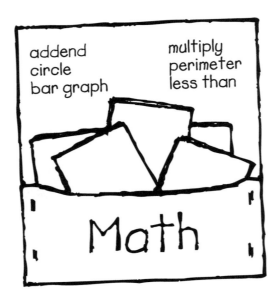

Sound Punctuation

by Doug and Sharman Wurst

▶ **Materials:** familiar children's books, chart paper, marking pen

▶ **Here's How!**

1. Write punctuation marks on the chart paper. Depending on the level of your students, use three or more of the following: period, question mark, exclamation mark, comma, quotation marks, apostrophe, and dash.

2. Have students assign a different sound to each punctuation mark. For example:

   period—honk
   question mark—meow
   exclamation mark—bang

3. Have pairs of students read from their reading books or library books, indicating punctuation marks by making the corresponding sounds. Be prepared for lots of laughs.

Dennis ran into the backyard. (honk) What was that in the maple tree? (meow) "Yikes!" (bang) he thought. "It looks awfully big!" (bang)

What's the Correct Ending Mark?

by Doug and Sharman Wurst

▶ **Materials:** index cards, pencils

▶ **Here's How!**

1. Give each student three index cards.

2. The student writes a period on the first card, a question mark on the second card, and an exclamation mark on the third card.

3. Read aloud one sentence found in the box below, using the proper inflection.

4. Students hold up appropriate punctuation cards, indicating the correct end mark for each sentence.

What color shirt is Mark wearing today?
Jonathan, there's a spider on your arm!
When will I get all my work done?
I'm wearing brown shoes today.
I won't sit down and you can't make me!
You are standing on one foot.
Why are you standing on one foot?
Stop standing on one foot!
Do you want to go swimming with me?
You can go swimming with me.
There's the water slide!
What did she say?
You must talk with me!
I went walking in a park and saw a goose.
The goose started to fly.
The goose started to chase me!
Why did the goose do that?
Do you like to sing?
I love to sing!
We will have choir practice today.
Will we have choir practice today?

Go Fish for Tens

by Susan Kunze

▶ **Materials:** a supply of number cards

▶ **Here's How!**

1. In advance, prepare cards numbered 0 through 9. You will need two or three sets per student. The box below gives three ways to make the cards. Although this may go against the grain of those of you who require order, it works just fine to dump all the cards needed for the entire class into a box and have students grab a bunch at the time of the activity.

2. Divide students into groups of two to four. Each group takes a large pile of cards. One player deals seven cards to each player. The rest of the cards are stacked in a pile.

3. The game is played like "Go Fish." Each player looks at his or her cards and lays down any pairs that add up to 10.

4. To begin play, the dealer asks another player for a card with a number that will allow him or her to make a pair with the sum of 10. If that player has the card asked for, he or she must give it to the requesting player. If not, he or she says, "Go fish," and the requesting player takes a card from the pile to add to his or her hand. If the student is able to use that card to make a sum of 10, he or she gets another turn. If not, it is the next player's turn.

5. Play continues until one player has made all his or her cards into pairs or until no more pairs can be made. Then players count their pairs. The player with the most pairs wins.

Ways to Make Number Cards
- Use decks of playing cards with the face cards removed. One deck is enough for two players. Ask students to bring incomplete decks from home.
- Using a black marker, write the numbers 1 through 9 on index cards. Let students help make these.
- Divide a sheet of copy paper into nine equal-sized boxes. Write in the numerals 1 through 9. Reproduce two or three sheets for each student. Laminate and cut apart.

Say It Another Way

by Susan Kunze

▶ **Materials:** a supply of number cards

▶ **Here's How!**

1. In advance, prepare cards numbered 0 through 9. You will need two or three sets per student. The box below gives three ways to make the cards. Although this may go against the grain of those of you who require order, it works just fine to dump all the cards needed for the entire class into a box and have students grab a bunch at the time of the activity.

2. Divide students into pairs. Give each pair a pile of cards.

3. Each student takes seven cards. The remaining cards are stacked facedown between the two players.

4. Player 1 turns over the top two cards from the stack and lays them down for both to see. The players calculate the sum.

5. Players look at their own hands to see if they can find combinations of cards that will equal that sum. For example, if the total of the two cards is 12, a student could combine 6 and 6 to make 12 or even 4 and 2 and 3 and 3.

6. Cards equaling the sum are placed in a discard pile.

7. Two more cards are turned over from the stack, and play continues.

8. The first player to use all seven of his or her cards is the winner.

Ways to Make Number Cards

- Use decks of playing cards with the face cards removed. One deck is enough for two players. Ask students to bring incomplete decks from home.
- Using a black marker, write the numbers 1 through 9 on index cards. Let students help make these.
- Divide a sheet of copy paper into nine equal-sized boxes. Write in the numerals 1 through 9. Reproduce two or three sheets for each student. Laminate and cut apart.

Addition Facts Flip

by Susan Kunze

▶ **Materials:** supply of number cards

▶ **Here's How!**

1. In advance, prepare cards numbered 0 through 9. You will need two or three sets per student. The box below gives three ways to make the cards. Although this may go against the grain of those of you who require order, it works just fine to dump all the cards needed for the entire class into a box and have students grab a bunch at the time of the activity.

2. Choose a number you want your students to practice adding onto. Write it on the chalkboard.

3. Each pair of students has a supply of cards that they divide into two piles, placed facedown.

4. To play, each player turns over the top card of his or her pile and adds the number on the card to the target number. Each player gives the sum. The player with the greatest sum takes both players' cards and places them in a new pile.

5. Play continues as time permits, or until both piles of cards have been depleted. The winner is the player with the most cards in his or her new pile.

Ways to Make Number Cards

- Use decks of playing cards with the face cards removed. One deck is enough for two players. Ask students to bring incomplete decks from home.
- Using a black marker, write the numbers 1 through 9 on index cards. Let students help make these.
- Divide a sheet of copy paper into nine equal-sized boxes. Write in the numerals 1 through 9. Reproduce two or three sheets for each student. Laminate and cut apart.

Right on Target
by Doug and Sharman Wurst

▶ **Materials:** paper, pencils, chalkboard and chalk (optional)

▶ **Here's How!**

1. Select a target number. For example, 10.

2. Ask students, "How many equations can you make that have the answer of 10?" Any combination is acceptable—addition, subtraction, and use of multiple addends.

3. Have the students write equations on a sheet of paper. (Several students might also write the problems on the chalkboard.)

4. Repeat as time allows, using different target numbers.

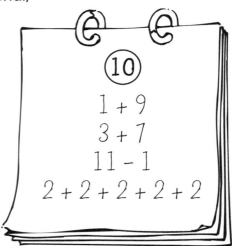

10

$1 + 9$
$3 + 7$
$11 - 1$
$2 + 2 + 2 + 2 + 2$

Bags of Beans

by Doug and Sharman Wurst

▶ **Materials:** a drawstring bag, 10 dried beans

▶ **Here's How!**

This is a great math activity to use after reading *Jack and the Beanstalk*.

1. Show students that you have 10 beans.

2. Put some of the beans in the bag.

3. Count with the class the number of beans that were **not** put in the bag.

4. Students determine how many beans are in the bag.

5. Repeat by putting a different number of beans in the bag or by starting with a different number of beans.

I have 10 beans.

How many are in the bag?

Clapping Sums
by Martha Cheney

▶ **Materials:** none

▶ **Here's How!**

This is a fun and different way to practice basic addition facts with young students. Students can sit at their desks or in a circle for this activity. (The circle is more fun!)

1. Call out a simple addition problem such as 3 + 2.

2. Students "clap" the answer with 5 claps. Demonstrate a steady, rhythmic beat so that everyone claps to the same rhythm.

3. Remind students not to say the answer aloud. Give students time to calculate before beginning to clap.

▶ **Variation**

Try this game with subtraction facts.

Shapely Sums
by Martha Cheney

▶ **Materials:** none

▶ **Here's How!**

1. Create addition problems using geometric shapes.

2. Ask students questions such as:

    How many sides are there on 2 squares?
    How many sides are there on 3 triangles?
    How many sides are there on 2 rectangles and 1 pentagon?

3. Introduce new shapes, such as hexagon, octagon, or trapezoid, to increase the difficulty level.

▶ **Variation**

Allow students to come to the chalkboard to draw solutions to the problems.

Boxes in Boxes

by Martha Cheney

▶ **Materials:** chalkboard, chalk

▶ **Here's How!**

1. Write this problem on the chalkboard:

   There are 3 large boxes.
   Inside each large box are
   2 small boxes.
   How many boxes in all?

2. Change the numbers of boxes in the problem. For example:

   There are 2 large boxes.
   Inside each large box are
   4 small boxes.
   How many boxes in all?

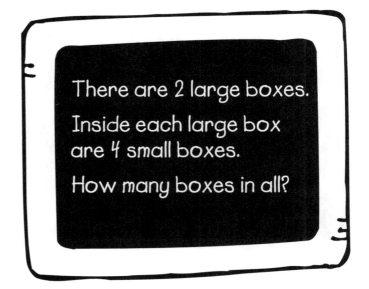

There are 2 large boxes.

Inside each large box are 4 small boxes.

How many boxes in all?

3. Add another level of difficulty by adding another size box to the problem. For example, there might be giant, large, small, and tiny boxes.

4. Ask students to brainstorm what might be inside the smallest boxes.

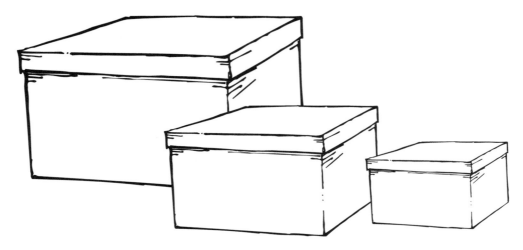

Adding On
by Susan Kunze

▶ **Materials:** chalkboard, chalk, one die for each pair of students, scratch paper, pencils

▶ **Here's How!**

1. Divide students into pairs. Determine a final score being aimed for and write it on the chalkboard.

2. The first player may roll the die as many times as desired. The number rolled each time is added to the previous total. **But**, if a 1 is rolled, all points accumulated on that turn are lost, and the player loses the turn.

3. When the first player chooses to stop or rolls a 1, the second player begins rolling. He or she may choose to stop rolling at any time and keep the points, but if a 1 is rolled, the points accumulated on that turn are lost.

4. Play continues until one player reaches the predetermined final score or until time is called.

Joe
5
+6
11
+2
13

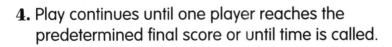

Tara
4
+3
7
+1
7

Generate a Sum

by Jennifer Prior

▶ **Materials:** a supply of number cards

▶ **Here's How!**

1. In advance, prepare cards numbered 0 through 9. You will need two or three sets per student. The box below gives three ways to make the cards. Although this may go against the grain of those of you who require order, it works just fine to dump all the cards needed for the entire class into a box and have students grab a bunch at the time of the activity.

2. Divide students into pairs. Give each pair a pile of cards.

3. To play, each student turns over the top two cards in his or her pile and adds them together.

4. The student whose sum is the greatest keeps all four cards.

5. Play continues until one student has no more cards left.

Ways to Make Number Cards
- Use decks of playing cards with the face cards removed. One deck is enough for two players. Ask students to bring incomplete decks from home.
- Using a black marker, write the numbers 1 through 9 on index cards. Let students help make these.
- Divide a sheet of copy paper into nine equal-sized boxes. Write in the numerals 1 through 9. Reproduce two or three sheets for each student. Laminate and cut apart.

Your cards equal 10. My cards equal 7. You take all of the cards.

Roll, Add, and Toss

by Susan Kunze

▶ **Materials:** dice, pennies, paper, pencils

▶ **Here's How!**

1. Students play in small groups. Each group uses two dice and a penny.

2. The first player rolls the dice, adds the numbers together, and records the sum.

3. Remaining players roll the dice, add the numbers together, and record their sums.

4. One player tosses the penny. Heads means the player with the greatest sum wins a point. Tails means the player with the lowest sum wins the point. If two players have the same winning sum, both receive a point.

5. Keep score until time is up. The player with the most points at the end of the game wins.

$$4 + 6 = 10$$

Number Crunchers

by Laurie Williams

▶ **Materials:** none

▶ **Here's How!**

1. Assign all students a different number, in sequence, beginning with 1.

2. Say a number sentence, such as "7 plus 5 equals." Students assigned those numbers stand.

3. All students should calculate the answer mentally.

4. The student assigned the number of the answer should stand.

5. Students standing say the equation aloud.

▶ **Variations**

• Play in the same manner, giving subtraction sentences.

• Have all students with even numbers stand. Say the numbers aloud in order.

• Have all students with odd numbers stand. Say the numbers aloud in order.

Handy Math Game

by Doug and Sharman Wurst

▶ **Materials:** paper, pencils

▶ **Here's How!**

1. Group students in pairs.

2. Partners pound their hands three times (as in "Rock, Paper, Scissors"). On the third pound, they extend 1, 2, 3, 4, or 5 fingers.

3. Students take turns adding the number of fingers showing. The other member of the pair records the sum.

4. Stop the game in time for the pairs to add up all of the recorded sums.

▶ **Variations**

* Older students may multiply the numbers represented on the fingers.

* Use this game to help young students visualize subtraction. To subtract numbers, students touch their fingers together. For example, if one student has 4 fingers up and the other student has 3 fingers up, when the fingers are matched one to one, the students discover that one finger is not touching. The answer is 1.

Roll and Subtract

by Susan Kunze

▶ **Materials:** three dice for each group, paper, pencils

▶ **Here's How!**

1. Students play in small groups. Each group uses three dice.

2. The first player rolls two dice and adds them together. Then he or she rolls the third die. The player subtracts the smaller number from the larger number and records the difference.

3. Each remaining player follows the same procedure.

4. Stop the game in time for students to add up all of the recorded differences. The player with the highest score is the winner.

▶ **Variation**

To practice subtraction facts to 18, give each group three dice. Players roll three dice together, add them together, and record the sum. Then players choose to roll one or two of the remaining dice, add the sum (if necessary), and then subtract the smaller number from the greater number.

$$4 + 6 = 10$$

3

$$\begin{array}{r} 10 \\ -\ 3 \\ \hline 7 \end{array}$$

Subtraction Facts Flip

by Susan Kunze

▶ **Materials:** a supply of number cards

▶ **Here's How!**

1. In advance, prepare cards numbered 0 through 9. You will need two or three sets per student. The box below gives three ways to make the cards. Although this may go against the grain of those of you who require order, it works just fine to dump all the cards needed for the entire class into a box and have students grab a bunch at the time of the activity.

2. Choose a target number and write it on the chalkboard.

3. Give each pair of students a supply of cards. Cards with a number higher than the target number are discarded. The remaining cards are placed in a stack between the two players.

4. To play, each player turns over a card from the stack. Each player subtracts his or her card number from the target number.

5. The player with the greatest difference takes both of the cards.

6. Play continues as time permits. The winner is the player with the greatest number of cards.

▶ **Variation**

To subtract from numbers larger than 9, use two cards to add up to the target number.

Ways to Make Number Cards
- Use decks of playing cards with the face cards removed. One deck is enough for two players. Ask students to bring incomplete decks from home.
- Using a black marker, write the numbers 1 through 9 on index cards. Let students help make these.
- Divide a sheet of copy paper into nine equal-sized boxes. Write in the numerals 1 through 9. Reproduce two or three sheets for each student. Laminate and cut apart.

Changing Signs

by Doug and Sharman Wurst

▶ **Materials:** chart paper, marker, paper, pencils

▶ **Here's How!**

1. Write several equations on the chart, omitting addition or subtraction signs. Make sure the top number is always larger than the bottom number. (See examples at right.)

2. Students add and then subtract each problem on paper.

▶ **Variation**

Write equations on the chalkboard that have answers, but are missing the addition or subtraction signs. Have students determine the missing signs.

Ten Fact Families

by Susan Kunze

▶**Materials:** small pieces of graph paper, pencils or crayons

▶**Here's How!**

1. Students outline ten squares on their graph paper and then color in as many of the squares as they choose.

2. Students record the fact family for the representation they have made. For example:

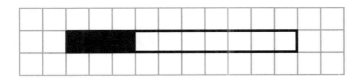

Three squares are shaded. Seven are not. The fact family would be:

$3 + 7 = 10$ $10 - 3 = 7$

$7 + 3 = 10$ $10 - 7 = 3$

3. By coloring in a different number of squares each time, students can make all the combinations of 10. These make great fact family flash cards!

▶**Variation**

Outline any number of squares and write the fact family for that number.

Multiplication Facts Flip

by Susan Kunze

▶ **Materials:** a supply of number cards

▶ **Here's How!**

1. In advance, prepare cards numbered 0 through 9. You will need two or three sets per student. The box below gives three ways make the cards. Although this may go against the grain of those of you who require order, it works just fine to dump all the cards needed for the entire class into a box and have students grab a bunch at the time of the activity.

2. Choose a target number and write it on the chalkboard.

3. Give each pair of students a supply of cards.

4. The students divide the cards in half and place them facedown between them.

5. Each player turns over a top card, multiplies it by the target number, and says the product.

6. The player with the greater product takes both cards.

7. Play continues as time allows or until both piles of cards have been depleted.

▶ **Variation**

To make this game easier, limit the cards that the students use (for example, use only the 1 through 5 cards).

Ways to Make Number Cards

• Use decks of playing cards with the face cards removed. One deck is enough for two players. Ask students to bring incomplete decks from home.
• Using a black marker, write the numbers 1 through 9 on index cards. Let students help make these.
• Divide a sheet of copy paper into nine equal-sized boxes. Write in the numerals 1 through 9. Reproduce two or three sheets for each student. Laminate and cut apart.

Generate a Product

by Susan Kunze

▶ **Materials:** three dice for each group, pennies, paper, pencils

▶ **Here's How!**

1. Divide students into small groups. Each group uses three dice and a penny.

2. The first player rolls two dice and adds them together. Then he or she rolls the third die, multiplies the sum by this number, and records the product.

3. Each remaining player follows the same procedure.

4. One player tosses the penny. Heads means the player with the greatest product wins a point. Tails means the player with the lowest product wins the point. If two players have the same winning product, both players receive a point.

5. Keep score until time is up. The player at the end of the game with the most points wins.

▶ **Variation**

To include practicing multiplication facts higher than the sixes, give each group four dice. Players roll two dice and add them. Players then choose to roll one or two of the remaining dice, add the sum (if necessary), and then multiply by the first sum.

$4 + 6 = 10$

3

$$\begin{array}{r} 10 \\ \times\ 3 \\ \hline 30 \end{array}$$

Guess the Operation

by Laurie Williams

▶ **Materials:** chart paper, marker

▶ **Here's How!**

1. Prepare a chart with the drawings and information shown below.

2. Announce three numbers in the order of a number sentence, leaving out the operation.

3. Students demonstrate the operation required in the number sentence by using body language.

Example 1:
You say, "3, 6, 18."
The students recognize that 3 x 6 = 18. They cross their arms, making an X for multiplication.

Example 2:
You say, "17, 12, 5."
The students recognize that 17 − 12 = 5. They hold their arms out straight for subtraction.

multiplication	subtraction	addition	division

| forearms crossed to make an X | arms out straight | hands making the plus sign | hands in fists one above the other about 3" apart |

Who's Eating School Lunch?
by Eve Timm

▶ **Materials:** none

▶ **Here's How!**

This is a great activity to do at the beginning of the day.

1. Have your class count the lunches brought from home.

2. Look to see who is absent and ask how many students are going home for lunch.

3. Ask the question, "How many students are eating a school lunch?"

4. When you have the correct answer ask, "How did you get your answer?"

Squared Shapes
by Susan Kunze

▶ **Materials:** 1" (2.5 cm) construction-paper squares, 1" graph paper, crayons

▶ **Here's How!**

1. Give each student four construction-paper squares and a piece of graph paper.

2. Have each student join the four squares along sides, not corners, to form as many different shapes as possible.

3. The student records each shape made by coloring it in on the piece of graph paper.

There are five possible shapes that can be made with four squares without duplicating any shape.

▶ **Variation**

Try this with five squares!

Whole-Body Skip Counting

by Doug and Sharman Wurst

▶ **Materials:** none

▶ **Here's How!**

1. Teach a rhythm for counting by 2s. For example:

stomp a foot, hands slap lap

2. Practice the rhythm and count each action aloud. Count as far as appropriate for your students.

stomp (1), slap (2), stomp (3), slap (4), stomp (5), slap (6), stomp (7), slap (8), etc.

3. Next, repeat the rhythm, mouthing the "stomp" number or saying them "in your head." Say only the "slap" numbers aloud.

stomp, slap (2), stomp, slap (4), stomp, slap (6), stomp, slap (8), etc.

4. When students have mastered counting by 2s, move on to patterns for other numbers. For example:

3s—stomp feet, hands slap lap, clap hands
4s—stomp feet, hands slap lap, clap hands,
    snap fingers
5s—stomp feet, hands slap lap, clap hands,
    snap fingers, nod head

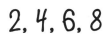

How Many Groups?

by Jennifer Norris

▶ **Materials:** none

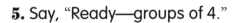

▶ **Here's How!**

1. Have all students stand quietly.

2. Announce a group size such as, "Groups of 3."

3. Students form into groups of 3. (Students remaining can choose a class mascot, a teacher, or a chair to complete the group.)

4. Point to one group at a time. Members of that group call out their numbers. For example, "3, 6, 9, 12," etc.

5. Say, "Ready—groups of 4."

6. Continue play as time allows.

Line Up

by Doug and Sharman Wurst

▶ **Materials:** none

▶ **Here's How!**

1. Ask your students to think about their birth dates. Ask, "What is the number of the day? Keep that number in your mind."

2. Have students line up by birth dates in ascending order (1, 2, 3, etc.) or descending order (31, 30, 29, etc.). The first time you do this, start with a small group of students. Gradually increase the size of groups. (Students with the same date should stand next to each other.)

3. Start at the front of the line and have students say their birth date in turn.

Where Am I in Line?

by Eve Timm

▶ **Materials:** wooden craft sticks, marking pen, empty coffee can

▶ **Here's How!**

1. Ahead of time, label each craft stick with a different number and store them in a coffee can. Use numbers appropriate to your students—from simple counting by ones to numbers in the hundreds and thousands for older students.

2. Pass out the sticks.

3. The students line up in numerical order according to the numbers on their sticks.

4. Repeat the activity as time allows, giving students a stick with a different number.

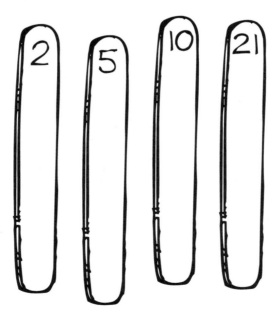

What Number Comes Before?

by Eve Timm

▶ **Materials:** none

▶ **Here's How!**

1. Announce a random number between 1 and 100.

2. Have the class tell you what number comes right before it. To maximize participation, have students share their answer with a neighbor before you call on a student to give the answer.

3. Continue by announcing another number.

▶ **Variation**

Play the same game by asking students to tell what comes after the random numbers.

Walk This Way

by Laurie Williams

▶ **Materials:** none

▶ **Here's How!**

1. Have students line up shoulder to shoulder in an open area of the classroom. You may need to have several lines.

2. Say, "Pretend you are standing on a number line. You are at 7. How do you get to 9? Will you step forward or backward?"

3. Direct students to count and step forward to 9.

4. Ask, "How many steps forward did you go?"

5. Next, say, "You are at 9. How will you get to 3?"

6. Direct students to count and step backward to 3.

7. Ask, "How many steps backward did you go?"

8. Pose new problems as time allows. For example:

Students are lined up on 4—
   6 is the next number (everyone steps forward 2 steps)
   8 is the next number (everyone steps forward 2 steps)
   3 is the next number (everyone steps back 5 steps)
   3 is the next number (everyone remains still)
   2 is the next number (everyone steps back 1 step)

How Many Jelly Beans Do I Have?

by Eve Timm

▶ **Materials:** hundreds chart (optional)

▶ **Here's How!**

Having a hundreds chart available is handy when first doing this activity. You might also want to have a jar of jelly beans as a prop. Pass out several to each student at the end of the activity.

1. Ask the question, "How many jelly beans do I have if I have 2 more than ____?" (Fill in the blank with any number.)

2. Continue to ask the question, using random numbers from 1 to 100.

3. Make this more challenging by changing "2 more" to a larger number such as "5 more."

▶ **Variation**

Try the same activity using mental subtraction.

2 more than 56 is 58.
5 more than 32 is 37.

Body Patterns

by Doug and Sharman Wurst

▶ **Materials:** none

▶ **Here's How!**

1. Have students stand in a line. Tell the first student to remain standing and the next to sit. Ask the remaining students to continue the pattern.

2. After the students are in the pattern, tell them the pattern they created is ABAB.

3. Continue the activity using new patterns. (See the box below.)

> Other patterns could include combinations of standing, sitting, arms extended, lying on the floor, curled in a ball, facing forward/backward, etc. For example:
>
> sitting, standing, sitting, standing... (ABAB)
> arms to the side, arms to the side, arms crossed... (AABAAB)
> curled in a ball, standing, sitting... (ABCABC)

▶ **Variation**

Have small groups of students develop their own patterns and model them for the class. Ask the class to name the patterns.

Number Patterns

by Laurie Williams

▶ **Materials:** chalkboard, chalk

▶ **Here's How!**

1. Begin by writing a number pattern on the chalkboard. (See the example at right.)

2. Have pairs of students work together to name the missing numbers and identify the pattern.

3. Ask a student to write the missing numbers on the board.

4. Write a different pattern on the board and continue in the same manner. For more difficult patterns, you may want to solve the patterns as a class.

Number Pattern Examples

Numbers	Next 3 #'s	Pattern
4, 6, 8, _, _, _	10, 12, 14	counting by 2s, even numbers
10, 15, 20, _, _, _	25, 30, 35	counting by 5s
1, 3, 5, _, _, _	7, 9, 11	counting by 2s, odd numbers
18, 15, 12, _, _, _	9, 6, 3	subtracting 3
5, 15, 25, _, _, _	35, 45, 55	adding 10
49, 48, 46, 43, _, _, _	39, 34, 28	subtracting 1, subtracting 2, subtracting 3…

▶ **Variation**

For harder activities, use multiplication and division in the pattern.

Pretty Patterns
by Laurie Williams

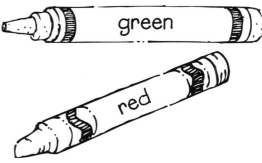

▶ **Materials:** paper, crayons

▶ **Here's How!**

1. Direct students to take out two crayons of different colors.

2. Tell students that they are going to create and label patterns made only from circles of these two colors. Challenge them to create as many different patterns as they can within the time allotted.

3. Stop the activity in time to allow students to share and compare their patterns with a neighbor.

Shape Patterns

by Marilyn Evans

▶ **Materials:** chalkboard, chalk, paper, pencils

▶ **Here's How!**

1. Draw three different shapes on the chalkboard. Choose those that your students are learning.

2. Challenge students to create as many patterns as they can using these shapes. They may repeat a shape as many times as desired.

3. Stop after a specific amount of time, say 4 to 5 minutes.

4. Have several students share a pattern. Draw students' patterns on the board and ask the class to label them. For example:

5. If time allows, have students label their own patterns.

Even and Odd

by Jennifer Norris

▶ **Materials:** none

▶ **Here's How!**

1. Have students stand in pairs.

2. Say a number.

3. If the number is odd, students move apart. If the number is even, students stay together.

▶ **Variation**

Give a number sentence. Students respond to show whether the answer is odd or even.

More or Less

by Martha Cheney

▶ **Materials:** beanbag or sponge ball

▶ **Here's How!**

1. Name a number.

2. Toss the beanbag to a student while calling out the word *more* or *less.*

3. The student should catch the beanbag and give a number that is more or less than the original number stated, depending on the command.

4. The student throws the beanbag to another student, again calling out *more* or *less.*

5. The game continues as time allows.

▶ **Variation**

Use the same framework to practice other math concepts. Toss the beanbag to a student while giving a basic multiplication problem, such as 4 x 5. The student must answer correctly and then throw the beanbag to another student while giving another multiplication problem.

High/Low Dice Throw

by Doug and Sharman Wurst

▶ **Materials:** chalkboard, chalk, three dice, paper, pencils

▶ **Here's How!**

1. Roll three dice.

2. Choose a student to write the numbers on the chalkboard, one on top of the other. (See the example at right.)

3. Have students write the largest and the smallest numbers that could be made by combining the digits (highest—641, lowest—146).

4. Ask place value questions such as, "For what place is the number the same?" (tens) "What number is in the hundreds place in this number?" (Point to one of the answers.)

5. Roll the dice again and continue in the same manner.

▶ **Variations**

• For young students, use only two dice.

• For older students, use four, five, or six dice.

• Use an eight-sided die.

Musical Numbers

by Laurie Williams

▶ **Materials:** paper, black crayons or marking pens, radio or tape recorder

▶ **Here's How!**

1. Place seven empty chairs side by side in the front of the classroom.

2. Have each student write any one-digit number on a sheet of paper.

3. Choose seven students to walk around the chairs while music plays, carrying the papers with the one-digit numbers written on them.

4. When the music stops, students sit in the chairs and hold up their numbers so that the class may see them.

5. The class reads the seven-digit number aloud.

6. Continue the play with seven new students.

Example
Students sit down with numbers 2, 5, 1, 7, 9, 4, and 2.
The number would be 2,517,942.
The class would read the number this way:
"two million, five hundred seventeen thousand, nine hundred and forty-two."

2,517,942

Comparing Hundreds

by Susan Kunze

▶ **Materials:** 30 small paper plates, marking pens (red, blue, and green)

▶ **Here's How!**

1. In advance, write a different number, 0 through 9, in red marker on 10 of the plates. Then do the same on the next 10 plates, using a blue marker. Make the third set of plates the same way, using a green marker.

2. To play, pass out the plates to your students. Some may have more than one plate, which will not affect the game.

3. Call out three combinations of numbers and colors. For example, "red two, blue four, and green seven."

4. Ask those students to stand in front of the class with their plates and make the greatest number possible (742). Engage the class in determining whether this is the correct answer.

5. Ask those students to form the least number possible (247) as well.

6. Play again by choosing three more color/number combinations.

▶ **Variation**

To play with thousands, make a fourth set of plates in another color.

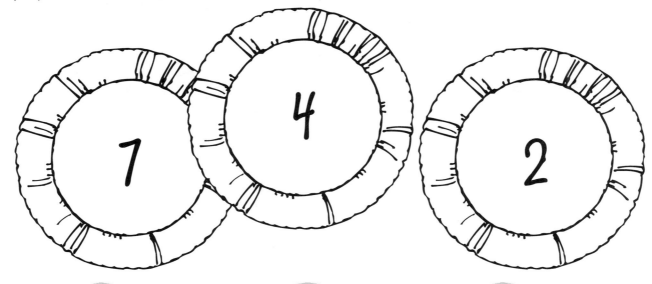

Tens and Ones Toss-Up

by Susan Kunze

▶ **Materials:** nine wooden craft sticks for every two students, marking pens or crayons, rubber bands, paper, pencils

▶ **Here's How!**

1. In advance, prepare the craft sticks. You may want students to do this as a separate 10-minute activity.

   - Give each pair of students nine craft sticks.
   - Have students make ten dots on one side of each craft stick and one dot on the other side of each stick.
   - Band the nine sticks together with a rubber band.

2. To play the game, divide students into pairs. Give one bundle of marked sticks to each pair.

3. Each player in turn gently tosses the sticks on a desk.

4. The player names the number tossed. For example, "4 tens and 5 ones is 45."

5. After each player has taken a toss, the player with the larger number gets a point.

6. The player with the most points at the end of the game wins.

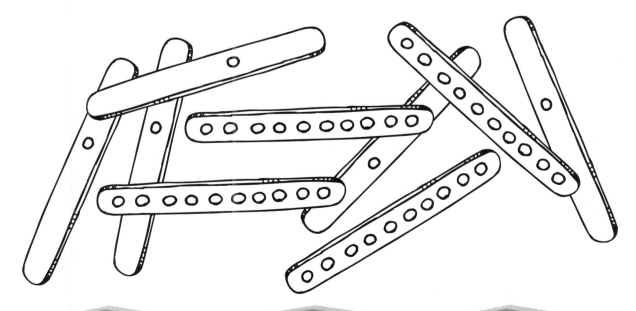

Playing with Place Value

by Martha Cheney

▶ **Materials:** index cards numbered 0 to 9

▶ **Here's How!**

Place value is a difficult concept for some students. Here is a fun way to reinforce their understanding.

1. Call two students to the front of the class.

2. Give each student a number card to hold.

3. Say a number that can be formed from the numerals on their cards. Challenge them to stand in the order needed to display the number you gave. For example, "63" or "36."

4. Ask the class to give "thumbs up/thumbs down" to indicate if the answer is correct.

5. Ask each of the two students to tell whether they are standing in the tens place or the ones place.

6. Have the students switch places. Ask the class to name the new number formed.

▶ **Variation**

Use additional cards to form three- or four-digit numbers if your students are ready.

Round Up & Round Down

by Laurie Williams

▶ **Materials:** two bells or buzzers

▶ **Here's How!**

1. Divide the class into two groups.

2. Appoint one student to be scorekeeper.

3. Each group forms a single-file line.

4. Invite the first two students in each line to the front of the classroom to compete against each other.

5. Place the bells or buzzers on a table in front of the two students.

6. Announce that you want the students to round two-digit numbers to the nearest ten and three-digit numbers to the nearest hundred.

7. The students stand with their hands behind their backs while you say the number "78."

8. The first student to ring in and correctly answer "80" wins one point for his or her team.

9. Those two students go to the back of the line, and the next two students come up. Then say, "336."

10. The students, hearing a three-digit number, must round to the nearest hundred and be the first to ring in with "300."

11. The team with the most points at the end of the playing time is the winner.

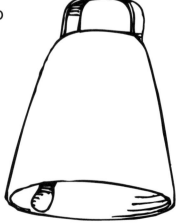

More Money

by Martha Cheney

▶ **Materials:** paper, pencils

▶ **Here's How!**

This activity helps students grasp the relative value of coins.

1. Pose a question such as:

Which is more, 15 dimes or 5 quarters?
Which is more, 120 pennies or 25 nickels?
Which is more, 30 nickels or 12 dimes?

2. Have students solve the questions, using pencil and paper. Suggest that students draw pictures if needed to help solve the problem.

3. Create new questions that are appropriate to the ability and experience of your students.

The Money in My Pocket
by Eve Timm

▶ **Materials:** none

▶ **Here's How!**

1. Tell students that you have some coins in your pocket. You will tell them what the coins are, and they are to tell you how much money you have. For example:

    1 nickel, 4 pennies—9¢

2. Continue in this manner with different coin combinations. Start with easy combinations using coins your students are familiar with. Move on to harder combinations. For example:

    3 nickels—15¢
    2 nickels, 2 pennies—12¢
    2 dimes, 1 nickel—25¢
    2 dimes, 1 nickel, 3 pennies—28¢

▶ **Variation**

Name a combination of coins. Have students calculate the sum. Then tell the students that one coin was lost. Have them subtract to find the new sum.

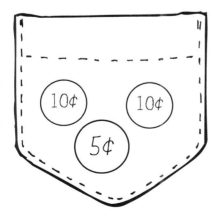 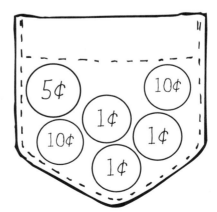

Buying Jelly Beans

by Doug and Sharman Wurst

▶ **Materials:** none

▶ **Here's How!**

1. Tell students that they will be asked to answer questions about buying jelly beans.

2. Say, "A jelly bean costs 2¢."

3. Then ask questions such as:

> If you have 6¢, how many jelly beans can you buy? (3)
> If you have 10¢, how many jelly beans can you buy? (5)
> If you have 14¢, how many jelly beans can you buy? (7)
> If you have 15¢, how many jelly beans can you buy? (7) "Will you have any
> money left over? How much? (Yes, 1¢)

4. Change the cost of a jelly bean and ask additional questions. For example,
   "A jelly bean costs 5¢."

> If you have 10¢, how many jelly beans can you buy? (2)
> If you have 30¢, how many jelly beans can you buy? (6)
> If you have 28¢, how many jelly beans can you buy? (5 jelly beans, 3¢ left over)

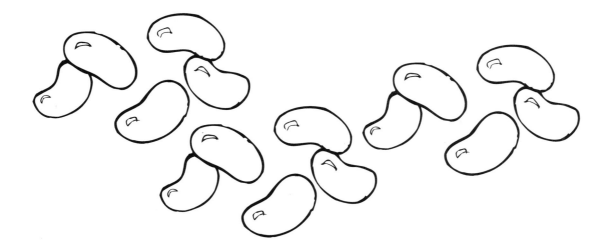

Bead a Necklace

by Susan Kunze

▶ **Materials:** chalkboard, chalk, crayons, paper

▶ **Here's How!**

1. Explain that you will be pretending to have a bead store.

2. On the chalkboard, list the inventory and prices of beads in your store. (See the example at right.)

3. Tell students that their challenge is to draw a necklace that costs 25¢.

4. Below their drawings, students should write the equation that shows the sum of their beads.

5. If time allows, let students share their solutions or draw another necklace that costs 25¢.

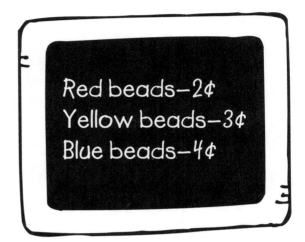

Red beads—2¢
Yellow beads—3¢
Blue beads—4¢

▶ **Variations**

* To make this easier, have students design a necklace and then calculate the total spent to make it. You can also adjust the cost of the beads to 1¢, 2¢, and 3¢.

* To make this more challenging, adjust the cost of the beads and the target total to higher numbers. Or, require that the beads form a pattern.

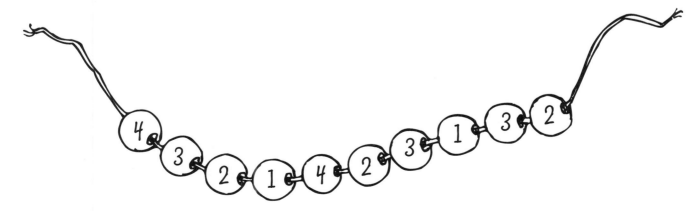

Digit Measurement
by Doug and Sharman Wurst

▶ **Materials:** paper, pencils

▶ **Here's How!**

1. Have students use their index fingers to measure the length of items at their desks—books, papers, pencils, crayons, etc.

2. Students write the name of the item and the item's length. For example, "the length of a math book is 4 fingers." Students may need to use fractions to give a more accurate measurement. For example, "the length of a math book is 4 ½ fingers."

3. Compare various students' measurements for the same items. Ask why there are differences.

▶ **Variations**

- Have students measure the perimeter of the same items.

- Have students measure objects with other nonstandard units of measure such as paper clips, blocks, or math manipulatives.

Estimation Jar

by Jennifer Norris

▶ **Materials:** clear container, small objects, adhesive notes

▶ **Here's How!**

1. Before the activity, fill a clear container with small objects such as marbles, paper clips, pennies, or rubber bands. Put in a number appropriate for the ability of your students. Count the objects as they're put in the container.

2. Hold the container up in front of the class.

3. Have students write "guesstimates" along with their names on adhesive notes.

4. Then have students attach their adhesive notes to the chalkboard.

5. Count the items aloud and determine a winner.

6. Discuss why some guesstimates were reasonable and others were not.

7. Repeat the activity using a different object—point out the size of the first object and the number needed to fill the container. Have students use this information to make estimates for the new object.

Give Me an Estimate
by Martha Cheney

▶ **Materials:** objects for counting (pennies or large dried lima beans)

▶ **Here's How!**

1. Have students sit in a circle on the floor.

2. Take a large handful of the counting objects and toss them gently into the center of the circle.

3. Ask a student to estimate the number of objects.

4. Encourage a very quick answer, as counting is not allowed.

5. Take estimates from two or three different students.

6. Count as a group to see how close the estimates were.

7. Continue playing, using different numbers of objects to estimate.

▶ **Variation**

As students gain skill, use larger numbers of objects.

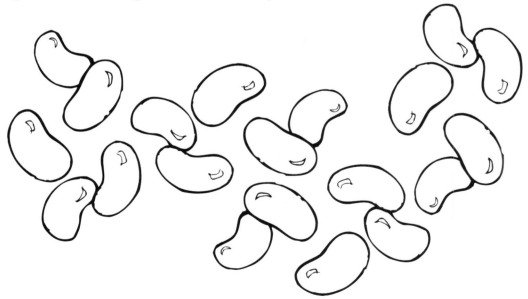

Flamingo Folly

by Doug and Sharman Wurst

▶ **Materials:** chalkboard, chalk, stopwatch or clock with a second hand

▶ **Here's How!**

1. Ask several students to predict how long they can stand on one foot. Have the class choose the prediction they think is most correct. Write that prediction on the chalkboard.

2. Have all students stand on one foot without any support.

3. Time the students until no one remains standing on one foot.

4. Write the time on the board. Compare the prediction to the actual time. Compute the difference.

▶ **Variations**

- Conduct the activity several times. Make a line graph of the results.

- Time students while balancing books on their heads or balancing pencils on their noses.

I Spy a Shape

by Doug and Sharman Wurst

▶ **Materials:** chalkboard, chalk

▶ **Here's How!**

1. Name a two-dimensional shape (square, for example). Draw that shape on the chalkboard. If your students are just learning the shape, point out an object in the classroom that has that shape.

2. Have students spy things in the classroom that are that shape.

3. Call on several students to name their object and tell how they know the object is that shape.

4. As time allows, have students find other shapes.

Classroom Shapes

square—desk top, floor tile, window, file drawer front
rectangle—chalkboard, pencil box
circle—holes in a pencil sharpener, clock
triangle—the inside of the capital letter *A*

▶ **Variation**

Have students find three-dimensional shapes (cylinder, cube, or sphere). Students stand near any shape of their choice. The teacher or leader names a shape. Those standing by that shape say, "Here's one!"

I Spy

by Laurie Williams

▶ **Materials:** none

▶ **Here's How!**

1. Secretly select an object in the classroom.

2. Describe it using only geometric shapes and approximate height, length, or width in standard or metric measurement.

3. Students attempt to guess the object.

Shape Up

by Laurie Williams

▶ **Materials:** small pieces of paper, black crayons

▶ **Here's How!**

1. Begin this activity by naming a geometric shape.

2. Each student draws the shape and writes the number of sides and holds the paper up for you to see.

3. Now name two geometric shapes, such as "pentagon and triangle."

4. Instruct students to draw both shapes, write the number of sides of both shapes, and add these numbers together.

5. Students hold up their papers for you to see.

6. Continue with new problems as time allows. For example:

     triangle + octagon = (11)
     square + rectangle = (8)
     hexagon + square = (10)

▶ **Variations**

- Try the same activity, asking students to perform subtraction of the sides.

- Give students an answer and challenge them to tell what shapes could be added to get that answer. For example:

     You: " The answer is 9."
     Students: "triangle + triangle + triangle" or "hexagon + triangle"

Sorting Sweets
by Martha Cheney

▶**Materials:** assortment of small wrapped candies (different colors, flavors, and shapes)

▶**Here's How!**

Sorting and classifying are good critical-thinking skills. Here is a quick way to practice.

1. Have your students sit in a circle.

2. Pass one candy to each student. Students are to place the candies on the floor in front of them.

3. Tell the students that they are going to sort the candies by color. Ask all students with red candies to place them in the center.

4. With the students' help, check to see that candies have been sorted correctly.

5. Allow students to retrieve their candies.

6. Ask for additional suggestions for sorting the candies. Possibilities include shape and flavor.

7. Allow students to eat the candy when the activity is finished.

Note: Be sure to determine in advance whether any students have food allergies or dietary restrictions.

Guess a Number

by Jennifer Norris

▶ **Materials:** scrap of paper, pencil, chalkboard, chalk

▶ **Here's How!**

1. Write a number on a piece of paper and describe the number to the class. For example, "It's between 1 and 100."

2. A student guesses a number.

3. You tell whether the mystery number is greater than or less than the number guessed.

4. Students continue guessing as the limits are narrowed until the correct number is guessed. To assist students in remembering the clues, record each guess on the chalkboard and write ">" or "<" next to the number.

> 45
> 90
< 82
> 75
> 80

Example

Teacher	Student
"The number is between one and one hundred."	"45"
"The number is greater than 45."	"70"
"The number is greater than 70."	"82"
"The number is less that 82."	"75"
"The number is greater than 75."	"80"
"The number is greater than 80."	"81"
"Yes, the number is 81!"	

Curly Q's

by Jill Norris

▶ **Materials:** chalkboard, chalk, paper, pencils (optional)

▶ **Here's How!**

1. Draw these figures on the chalkboard:

2. Tell students that the figures are called Curly Q's. Ask students to look closely at the Curly Q's. What characteristics do they have in common? (circle face, two eyes, one curlicue, and a body)

3. Draw each of these figures on the board, one at a time. Tell students that the figure is **not** a Curly Q. Ask, "Why isn't it a Curly Q?"

    It has a mouth.   It has two curlicues.   It has a square face.

4. Draw each of these figures on the board, one at a time. Ask students to determine if each is a Curly Q and tell why or why not.

      Yes.   No, it has a smile.   No, it has no curlicue.

5. As time permits, allow students to draw their own figures (either Curly Q's or not) and share them with a partner. You might post all the drawings later so that the class can determine which are Curly Q's.

When Is It?

by Martha Cheney

▶**Materials:** none

▶**Here's How!**

Use this activity to develop logical thinking. As a bonus, it will help students remember important dates.

1. Choose a month. Give a series of clues that will help students narrow the field until they are able to identify the month. For example:

   • This month is not in the winter.
   This month has 31 days.
   This is the month when we celebrate Columbus Day.
   Sometimes we dress in funny costumes in this month.
   (October)

   • It may be hot in this month.
   Students may be on summer vacation during this month.
   This month begins with the first letter of the alphabet.
   The month has six letters in its name.
   (August)

2. If your students are ready, give clues for a specific day. For example:

   • This date occurs in the summer.
   The month does **not** begin with the letter A.
   This date has two digits.
   The sum of the two digits is 5.
   This date occurs in a month with 30 days.
   This date occurs in the first half of the month.
   (June 14, Flag Day)

   • This is a fun holiday.
   This special day began in Ireland.
   The color green is associated with this day.
   There are stories about tricky little men with pots of gold.
   (March 17, St. Patrick's Day)

Instant Graph

by Martha Cheney

▶ **Materials:** adhesive notes, chart paper, marker

▶ **Here's How!**

1. Post the chart paper in front of the class.

2. Determine the topic for your graph. Perhaps you would like to create a graph showing what the students had for lunch. You know that the cafeteria served a choice of pizza or chicken. You also know that some students brought their lunches from home. Write the choices along one edge of the chart paper—pizza, chicken, sack lunch.

   Allow each student to come forward and place an adhesive note next to the correct category.

▶ **Variation**

Other possible topics for instant graphs include students' bedtimes, methods of transportation to school, favorite colors, pets, etc.

Candy Math

by Laurie Williams

▶ **Materials:** jar of small candies (M & Ms®, Skittles®, or jelly beans), graph paper,
    crayons

▶ **Here's How!**

1. Divide students into pairs.

2. Distribute a handful of candies to each pair of students.

3. Have students separate the candies into colors.

4. Instruct students to construct a graph on their paper, coloring in one square (with
   a corresponding color of crayon) for each color of candy.

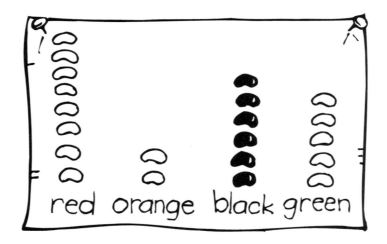

Paper Poll
by Doug and Sharman Wurst

▶ **Materials:** paper, pencils, chalkboard, chalk

▶ **Here's How!**

1. Have each student write the name of a favorite zoo animal on a piece of paper.

2. Ask one student to tell the name of the animal he or she selected.

3. Ask everyone who has the same animal to stand.

4. Record the name of the animal and the number of students who chose it on the chalkboard.

5. Continue this process until everyone's animal has been recorded on the board.

6. Use the information to make a graph on the board. If more time is available, have students make the graph on their papers.

Other Categories to Use
favorite music groups, TV shows, athletic teams, cartoon characters, foods, desserts, or colors

Grid Lock

by Douglas and Sharman Wurst

▶ **Materials:** masking tape, marking pen, two dice, chalkboard, chalk

▶ **Here's How!**

1. In advance, place a small piece of masking tape on each side of the dice. Use a marking pen to label each side of one die with a different letter, A through F. Label the second die with a different number, 1 through 6.

2. On the chalkboard, draw a grid as shown below, omitting the X.

3. Have a student roll the letter die and announce the letter on the top.

4. Have a second student roll the number die and announce the number on the top.

5. Ask another student to draw an X on the grid at the intersection of the letter and number rolled. Ask for "thumbs-up" or "thumbs-down" to assess class agreement on the placement of the X.

6. Continue in this manner as time permits.

Fact or Opinion?

by Douglas and Sharman Wurst

▶ **Materials:** none

▶ **Here's How!**

After learning about any historical figure, review the information learned and practice distinguishing between fact and opinion at the same time.

1. Give one statement at a time. (Suggestions for several historical figures are given below. Add others of your choosing.)

2. Instruct students to remain seated if the statement is a fact and stand if the statement is an opinion.

Martin Luther King, Jr.
Martin Luther King, Jr. was an African American. (fact)
Martin Luther King, Jr. was born on January 15, 1929. (fact)
Martin Luther King, Jr. was the most important civil rights leader. (opinion)
Martin Luther King, Jr. gave his "I Have a Dream" speech on August 28, 1963. (fact)
Martin Luther King, Jr.'s "I Have A Dream" speech was his most important speech. (opinion)
Martin Luther King, Jr. was the first African American to receive the "Man of the Year" award from *Time* magazine. (fact)
Martin Luther King, Jr. was the best choice for the "Man of the Year" award from *Time* magazine. (opinion)

George Washington
George Washington was the first president of the United States. (fact)
George Washington was the best president in the history of the United States. (opinion)
George Washington lived at Mount Vernon, Virginia. (fact)
George Washington always told the truth. (opinion)
George Washington was the best man to be the first president. (opinion)
George Washington commanded the colonial army during the American Revolution. (fact)

The Pilgrims
The Pilgrims would have all died without Squanto's help. (opinion)
The Pilgrims should have sailed farther south where it was warmer. (opinion)
The first winter brought many hardships for the Pilgrims. (fact)
The native people taught the Pilgrims how to grow corn. (fact)
Corn, beans, and squash are the best foods to grow. (opinion)

On the Mayflower or Now?

by Douglas and Sharman Wurst

▶ **Materials:** none

▶ **Here's How!**

As a part of culminating your Thanksgiving studies, ask students to determine which items would have been found on the Mayflower and which are modern items.

1. Read one item in the box below.

2. Have students stand if the item could have been on the Mayflower and sit if the item could not have been on the Mayflower.

3. Continue in this manner, having students respond to each item on the list. Briefly discuss students' responses.

4. Invite students to pose additional items for the class to respond to.

flour/sugar/salt	chain saw
canned food	hatchet
frozen food	flashlight
wool/cotton clothes	sleeping bags
electric blanket	propane camp stove
tennis shoes	cell phone
baseball cap	matches
bonnet	paper and writing implements
plastic rain poncho	radio
deck of cards	handheld electronic game

Name That Holiday
by Douglas and Sharman Wurst

▶ **Materials:** none

▶ **Here's How!**

1. Challenge your students to try to identify a holiday from a set of clues. Read the clues from the box below one at a time.

2. Encourage students to guess the holiday based on the clues. Allow only one guess per student, per holiday.

New Year's Day—football games, you stayed up late the night before, it is a first, you make resolutions

Flag Day—it is a holiday that represents something filled with stars; waving; red, white, and blue; Old Glory

Fourth of July—parades, outdoor picnics, independence, you get a bang out of it

Thanksgiving—parades, always on a Thursday, Pilgrims/Native Americans, turkey

Martin Luther King, Jr. Day—parades, speeches, for a national leader, dedicated to an African-American man

Veterans Day—parades, flags, uniforms, honoring military people

Arbor Day—spring, planting, trees

Abraham Lincoln's Birthday—honesty, freedom for all, log cabin, 16th president

George Washington's Birthday—soldier, Revolutionary War, Mount Vernon, Father of His Country

All in the Family

by Jill Norris

▶ **Materials:** chalkboard, chalk, paper, pencils or crayons

▶ **Here's How!**

1. Ask students to define the word *relatives*.

2. After agreeing on a definition, brainstorm and list common relatives.

3. Show students how to create a simple family diagram. They write their names in the middle of the paper. In a circle around the edge, they list the names of family members that they know.

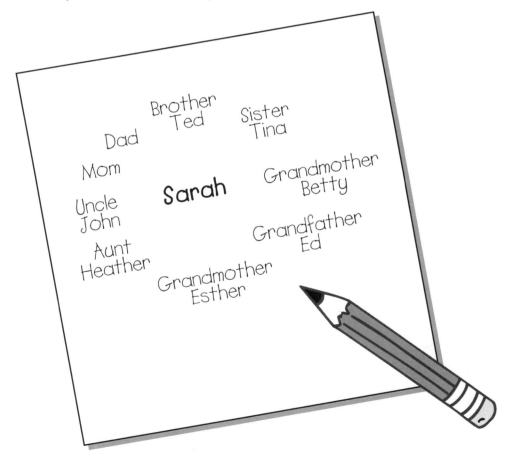

Chopsticks
by Doug and Sharman Wurst

▶**Materials:** a pair of chopsticks for each student or two pencils, crayons, pencil-top erasers or small math manipulatives

▶**Here's How!**

Chopsticks may be obtained at grocery stores or Chinese restaurants.

1. Explain that in many cultures, people use chopsticks as eating utensils.

2. Have students practice using chopsticks by picking up crayons, pencil-top erasers, or small math manipulatives.

▶**Variation**

After students have learned to use the chopsticks, incorporate their use into a relay race. Give each team one pair of chopsticks. Students pick up an object, carry it to a designated goal, and leave it there. They return with the chopsticks and hand them to the next student in line. This student uses the chopsticks to retrieve the object and return it to the starting point. Continue in this fashion until everyone on each team has completed a turn.

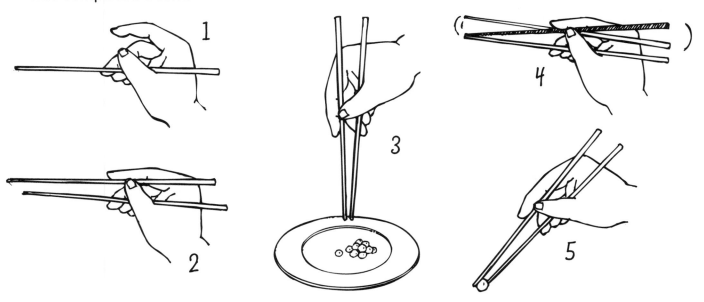

People in the World
by Doug and Sharman Wurst

▶ **Materials:** world map

▶ **Here's How!**

1. Using a world map, point out and name the continents listed in the box below.

2. Have students stand around the perimeter of the room. Say, "The desks are going to represent different continents in the world. Some of you are going to be asked to take your seats to show how many people live in a place compared to the amount of land."

3. Ask one student to take his or her seat. Tell the others, "This student represents the number of people who live in Australia. All of the desks represent the land in Australia." Point out Australia on the map once again.

4. Next, have three more students sit at their desks (for a total of four students sitting). Say, "These four students represent how many people live in North America. All of the desks represent the land in North America. Is North America more crowded than Australia?"

5. Continue this process until you get to Europe or Asia. If you do not have enough students to represent these continents, ask how many more students would have to join them at their desks.

6. Summarize the experience by asking questions such as:

   Which land area has the most room for people to move around?
   Which continent is the most crowded?
   Which continent is about as crowded as the one on which you live?

# of students at desks	
Australia	1
North America	4
South America	5
Africa	7
Europe	25
Asia	34

Calling All Captions
by Martha Cheney

▶ **Materials:** magazine pictures showing people engaged in various jobs, chart paper, marking pens

▶ **Here's How!**

1. Choose a picture to display. Tape it to a piece of chart paper.

2. Discuss the picture with students. Ask questions that address the main idea of the picture, such as:

   What is the person doing?
   What do we call that kind of job?
   What are the important things about the picture?

3. Work with students to devise a caption for the picture.

4. Tell students that a caption is a brief explanation of what is being shown in a picture.

5. Write the caption on the chart below the picture.

▶ **Variation**

Have older students write their own captions for the pictures.

Mad Dash for Trash

by Martha Cheney

▶ **Materials:** plastic bags

▶ **Here's How!**

Remind students that we all share responsibility for the world we live in. Everyone can, and should, help to keep our environment clean.

1. Divide students into pairs. Give each pair a large plastic trash bag.

2. Leave for lunch or recess 10 minutes early.

3. Have students make a quick tour around the play area or school grounds picking up litter.

4. Be sure to have students wash their hands before going to lunch.

5. Explain that they have just contributed to society in an important way.

Jump for Directions

by Susan Kunze

▶ **Materials:** *North, South, East, West* signs

▶ **Here's How!**

1. Make tagboard signs for *North, South, East,* and *West.*

2. Place the direction signs on the four walls in your classroom to indicate the approximate direction students are facing when looking at each wall.

3. Students stand and follow your oral directions such as:

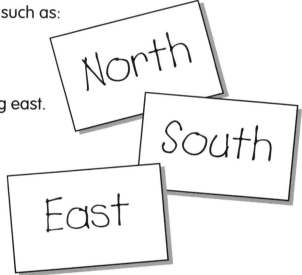

   Turn and face south.
   Take two steps to the west.
   Hop on one foot three times going north.
   Jump around in a circle until you are facing east.
   Crab crawl north until I say "Stop."
   Walk west for ten baby steps.
   Skip twice to the east.
   Shuffle your feet north until I say "Stop."
   Tiptoe south for four steps.
   Take one giant step south.
   Face east and touch your toes.
   Face west and touch your nose.

4. Continue improvising directions for your students until time runs out.

▶ **Variation**

You can make this more complex by placing four more signs in the corners of your room, indicating northeast, northwest, southeast, and southwest. Then give students oral directions that include them.

Direction Connection
by Laurie Williams

▶**Materials:** chalkboard, chalk, graph paper, pencils

▶**Here's How!**

1. On the chalkboard, demonstrate how students should draw intersecting lines labeled *North, South, East,* and *West* on the top half of the graph paper.

2. Have each student place his or her pencil tip on the end of the line near the N.

3. Call out a number of squares and a direction. For example, "Four east."

4. Each student draws a line over four squares to the east of the starting point. (You may want to demonstrate this on the chalkboard.)

5. Then call out another number and direction, "Two south."

6. The student starts where he or she ended the previous line and draws a line two squares to the south.

7. Continue in this manner, pausing periodically to be sure that all students are following along correctly. For example:

    one west
    two south
    four west
    four north
    one east

8. If time allows, do another drawing in the bottom half of the graph paper.

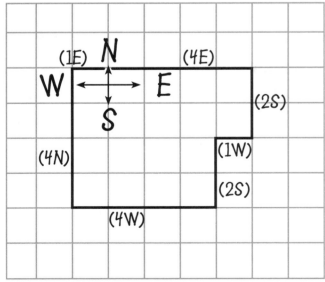

Community Helpers Password

by Laurie Williams

▶ **Materials:** chart paper, marker

▶ **Here's How!**

bus driver
nurse
doctor
dentist
librarian
plumber
carpenter
teacher
farmer

1. With your students, brainstorm and list familiar community helpers on the chart.

2. Divide the class into two teams. Tell them that you are going to give clues about one of the community helpers on the list. The team who guesses the helper first gets a point.

3. Select one student at a time to represent each team. Instruct the remaining team members to listen carefully so they are aware of all clues given.

4. Give a one-word clue to Team A's representative. The student has 10 seconds to guess the career or community helper.

5. If the student does not guess correctly, the representative of Team B gets to hear a second one-word clue and has 10 seconds to respond.

6. After every two clues, or whenever a team guesses correctly, choose a new representative from each team.

7. The team with the most points at the end of the playing period is the winner.

Example
Teacher says to Team A, "traffic."
Student from Team A guesses, "truck driver."
Teacher says to Team B, "uniform."
Student from Team B guesses, "nurse."
Teacher says to new student on Team A, "badge."
Student from Team A guesses, "police officer."
Teacher says, "Correct. Team A earns one point."

Who Helps Our Community?

by Jennifer Prior

▶ **Materials:** none

▶ **Here's How!**

1. Gather the students in a circle.

2. Begin by naming a community helper. The child beside you must tell what this helper does to assist the community.

3. That student then names another community helper and the student beside him or her tells how the helper contributes to the community.

4. Continue in this manner until every student in the circle has participated. Be ready to help out students who cannot think of a helper. You may want to have a list of helpers posted nearby.

Help Wanted

by Susan Kunze

▶ **Materials:** chalkboard, chalk, paper, pencils

▶ **Here's How!**

1. Write the information at right on the chalkboard.

2. Ask students to name an occupation. As a class, complete the help wanted ad. For example:

   Wanted: Fire fighter
   Must know how to:
      run fire trucks
      hook up hoses
      enter a burning building
      use an ax and a crowbar

Wanted:
_____

Must know how to:
_____
_____
_____

3. Ask each student to select an occupation with which he or she is familiar. Have each student write a want ad poster for the job, describing the skills needed.

Community Charades
by Martha Cheney

▶ **Materials:** none

▶ **Here's How!**

1. Have students sit in a circle.

2. Ask a volunteer to come to the center of the circle and pantomime the actions of a community member. This may be anyone who works in the community, such as a fire fighter, painter, doctor, carpenter, teacher, judge, etc.

3. Allow the student who guesses correctly to take the next turn.

"Is she using a saw?"
"She's a carpenter!"

Community Who Am I?

by Susan Kunze

▶ **Materials:** paper, pencils

▶ **Here's How!**

1. Encourage students to think about workers in their community. Where do they work? What kind of work do they do?

2. Working alone or in pairs, have students write riddles giving clues about one type of community worker.

   "I push a broom and use a vacuum, a sponge, and a bucket. I work in our school. Who am I?"

3. As each student or pair completes their riddle, have them trade with another student or pair and try to solve the riddle they have been given.

4. Keep writing and solving riddles as time allows.

I Can Help, Too!
by Jennifer Prior

▶ **Materials:** none

▶ **Here's How!**

1. Explain to your students that everyone is important in helping the school run smoothly.

2. Divide students into groups of three or four.

3. Tell students a scenario. (See the box below for suggestions.)

4. Have each group think of a way to deal with the situation and share their answers with the class.

5. After some experience responding to presented scenarios, ask students to suggest other situations.

Example Scenarios

You are working on a group project. One of your group members is not participating. What could you do or say to involve that student?

There is a new student in your class. On the playground this student is standing all alone. What could you do?

You are in the cafeteria. One of your classmates is making a mess on the table and floor. What could you do?

Two of your classmates are arguing at recess. How could you help them solve their problem?

You see an older student throwing paper on the ground. What could you do about it?

A teacher you don't know is carrying a big pile of books. He trips and the books go flying. What could you do?

Search the States

by Martha Cheney

▶ **Materials:** a large U.S. map

▶ **Here's How!**

1. Post a large U.S. map.

2. Gather students close to the map so that all can see.

3. Challenge students to find answers to the following questions by looking at the map.

> How many states begin with the letter M?
> Which state is farthest to the north?
> Which states border both Oregon and Arizona?
> Which state is the largest?
> Which state has Albany as its capital city?

▶ **Variation**

Use a world map to do a similar activity with older students.

My Expanding World

by Laurie Williams

▶ **Materials:** chalkboard, chalk

▶ **Here's How!**

1. Write the following categories on the chalkboard: *House, Neighborhood, City*.

2. Name items that might be found in the different places. (See the box below.)

3. Have students identify each item's category.

4. Write the item in the category or categories where it belongs.

5. Ask students to suggest additional items for each category.

House	Neighborhood	City
closet	streetlights	McDonalds
cookbook	sidewalks	city hall
bed	stop sign	department store
pets	playground	Y.M.C.A.
bicycle	backyards	police station
television	fences	library
		bank
		shopping mall
		gas station
		schools

On the Map

by Jill Norris

▶ **Materials:** chart paper, two colors of marking pens

▶ **Here's How!**

Landforms   Water Forms

1. Write the headings shown on the chart at right.

2. Divide students into two teams. Designate a colored marker for each team.

3. Teams take turns naming a landform or a water form. They must state which form they are naming. For example:

   landform—hill

4. Write each correct response on the chart using that team's color. If a response is incorrect, or a team cannot think of a response in a reasonable amount of time, the turn moves to the other team.

5. Count the responses of each color to determine the winning team.

Landforms
hill, mountain, valley, plateau, mesa, plain, peninsula, island, reef, delta, cape, bluff, cliff, volcano

Water Forms
ocean, sea, river, stream, pond, lake, bay, strait, gulf

Resourceful Graphing

by Susan Kunze

▶ **Materials:** chalkboard, chalk, paper, pencil

▶ **Here's How!**

1. Hold up a piece of paper and a pencil. Ask students to name the items. Ask, "What do these two thing have in common?" Guide the discussion to the conclusion that both are made from wood, which comes from trees.

2. Draw a graphic organizer on the chalkboard. Ask students to think of other products that come from trees.

3. If time allows, repeat the activity with other natural resources. For example:

   wheat, rubber, cows, steel or metal, chickens, cotton

Continent Spotlight

by Laurie Williams

▶ **Materials:** world map (optional)

▶ **Here's How!**

1. Name landmarks, bodies of water, or major geographical regions that are on a specific continent. You may want to display a world map.

2. The students try to guess which continent is being spotlighted.

3. The student who guesses correctly gets to think of a continent and give clues such as a country, a landmark, or a body of water.

Example

Teacher says, "France."
No students raise their hands to guess.
Teacher says, "Alps."
Student guesses, "Asia."
"Try again, that's not it," says the teacher, "Spain."
"Europe," guesses a student.
"Correct!" On a world map, the teacher identifies the continent Europe as well as France, the Alps, and Spain to show they are all in Europe.

Count in Japanese
by Doug and Sharman Wurst

▶**Materials:** chart paper or overhead transparency

▶**Here's How!**

1. In advance, make a chart or overhead transparency of the numbers 1 to 10 in Japanese.

2. Hold up the correct number of fingers and say the Japanese number.

3. Students repeat the number.

4. Continue in this manner with all 10 numbers.

5. Allow students to say any number they wish in Japanese. Classmates show the correct number of fingers.

Number	Word	How to Say
1	ichi	ee-chee
2	ni	nee
3	san	sahn
4	shi	shee
5	go	go
6	roku	ro-koo
7	shichi	shi-chee
8	hachi	hah-chee
9	ku	koo
10	ju	joo

Who Am I?

by Doug and Sharman Wurst

▶ **Materials:** list of clues (see box below)

▶ **Here's How!**

1. Prepare a list of clues that identify famous people in history with whom students are familiar. (Some samples are given below.)

2. Read clues one at a time.

3. Each student may guess a person's name only once.

Famous People in History

Sacajawea
She was born in 1784.
She was a member of the Shoshoni tribe.
She was also known as Bird Woman.
She helped lead the Lewis and Clark Expedition in the Pacific Northwest.
Her face is on the new United States dollar coin.

Martin Luther King, Jr.
He was born in 1929.
He was a pastor of a church.
He believed in nonviolence.
We celebrate his life in January.
He wrote the speech, "I Have a Dream."

Abraham Lincoln
He was born in 1809.
He was a lawyer.
He was born in a log cabin.
He was president during the Civil War.

George Washington
He was born in 1732.
He was a general.
He was a president of the United States.
He headed the Virginia delegation to the Constitutional Convention.
He had wooden teeth.

Away We Go

by Jill Norris

▶ **Materials:** chalkboard, chalk

▶ **Here's How!**

1. Brainstorm and list as many means of transportation as students can name. Encourage them to think about forms from times past as well as modern means.

2. Ask for suggestions for grouping the forms of transportation into categories. For example:

> where the form of transportation is used—land, air, water
> transportation of long ago/transportation of modern times
> method of propulsion—muscle, air, gasoline, steam, coal
> private transportation/public transportation

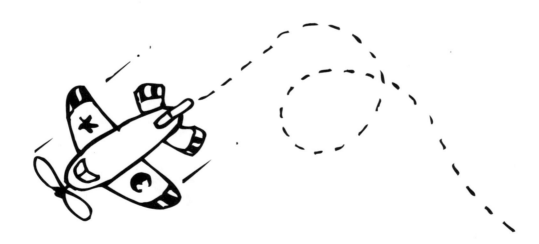

Needs or Wants
by Jill Norris

▶ **Materials:** chart paper, marker

▶ **Here's How!**

1. Construct a T chart on the chart, as shown at right.

2. Ask the class to help you define the meanings of the two words.

   Needs—things that you must have to live
   Wants—things that are nice to have

3. Ask students to name items and tell you under which heading to list them. You may need to guide students in naming some.

4. When you have compiled a reasonable list, have the class vote to evaluate the placement of each item.

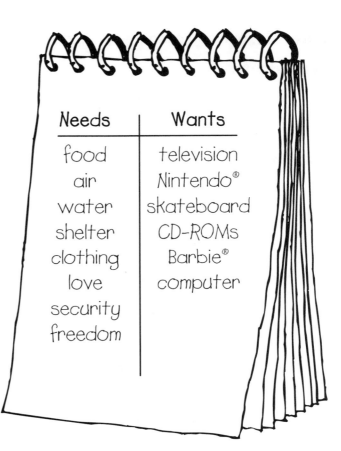

Needs	Wants
food	television
air	Nintendo®
water	skateboard
shelter	CD-ROMs
clothing	Barbie®
love	computer
security	
freedom	

What's in the Box?

by Doug and Sharman Wurst

▶ **Materials:** one can of soda, box, tape, chalkboard, chalk

▶ **Here's How!**

1. Place a can of soda in a box, making sure it can roll around.

2. Tape the box closed.

3. Show students the box and ask, "What do you think is in this box?"

4. Write student guesses on the chalkboard.

5. Ask, "Is there a way you could find out more about what's in this box without opening it?" Write student suggestions (shake, tilt, weigh, etc.) on the board. Tell students that scientists have a name for these manipulation ideas—indirect observation. This is because we cannot see the object directly.

6. Let students try all the manipulation ideas that they suggested.

7. Write any new guesses about the object's identity on the board.

8. When all guesses have been made, ask students if any of the guesses on the board should be eliminated and why.

9. Finally, have students vote on which of the guesses is most likely to be found in the box.

10. Open the box and have a discussion about indirect observation.

Adding Attributes

by Martha Cheney

▶ **Materials:** chart paper, marker

▶ **Here's How!**

This activity will help students understand the important concept of attributes.

1. Name an attribute. For example, you might name the color yellow.

2. Write *yellow* on the chart paper.

3. Beneath this, list yellow objects that students brainstorm. Allow 2 or 3 minutes for this task.

4. Next, name another attribute. For example, you might name the shape *round*.

5. Write *yellow* and *round* on the chart and list objects that have both attributes. Use objects from the first list and add other objects as well.

6. After each attribute, take a moment to discuss the students' ideas. Notice that the list of items generally becomes shorter as you add attributes. Ask students why this is so.

Food Pyramid Fun

by Marilyn Evans

▶ **Materials:** none

▶ **Here's How!**

When you line up for lunch, use this great follow-up activity to a unit about the food pyramid.

1. When students are in line for lunch, name one of the five food groups—grains, fruits and vegetables, meat, dairy, fats/oils/sweets.

2. Start at the front of the line and ask each student in order to name a food from that group. If a student cannot think of a food, he or she says, "Pass," and the next student in line attempts to name a food.

3. When no one can think of any more foods in that group, count the number of foods named. Record the number and attempt to break that record another time.

4. When you line up the next day, name foods from another food group.

Memory Games

by Doug and Sharman Wurst

▶ **Materials:** chalkboard, chalk, paper, pencils

▶ **Here's How!**

These two games help students learn how to use patterns and logical order to help them remember information or data. Each game can be a separate 10-minute activity.

Game One

1. Have a student come to the front of the class and stand facing the class for about 15 seconds.

2. The student then sits at the back of the class, where he or she cannot be seen.

3. Have the class name the details they can remember about what the student is wearing. Check the number and accuracy of the details remembered.

4. Then ask students to develop mental checklists, looking for items from head to toe. Do the activity again to see if their observations improve.

Game Two

1. Divide students into pairs.

2. Tell students that you are going to say a list of words for them to memorize. They are to memorize them in the order given: hamburger, drink, fork, plate, French fries, knife, napkin, spoon, apple pie, place mat.

3. Wait 15 seconds and ask students to recall with their partners as many words as possible. Ask if anyone was able to name all the words and in the same order.

4. Then tell students that you will put the words in a different order to see if anyone has an easier time remembering the words. Also tell them to visualize placing each item on a dinner table. Say the words in this order: place mat, napkin, knife, fork, spoon, plate, hamburger, French fries, drink, and apple pie.

5. Wait 15 seconds and ask pairs to recall the words. Have a discussion about the importance of putting information that needs to be memorized into a logical order.

Species Charades

by Laurie Williams

▶ **Materials:** slips of paper, jar

▶ **Here's How!**

1. Ahead of time, write the name of a different animal on each slip of paper. Here are some suggestions of animals that might be easy to pantomime:

    reptiles—turtle, lizard, Tyrannosaurus Rex, rattlesnake, boa constrictor
    amphibians—frog, toad
    birds—woodpecker, ostrich, hummingbird, vulture, eagle, flamingo, duck
    mammals—elephant, giraffe, cat, horse, dog, cow, bull, deer, lion, bear, sea lion
    fish—shark, manta ray, salmon (migrating), swordfish

2. Fold the slips and place them in a jar.

3. Select one student to take a piece of paper out of the jar.

4. The student silently acts out the animal.

5. Students guess the animal being portrayed and must also guess the species. For example, if a student guesses "elephant," he or she must also say "mammal."

6. Continue in this manner, allowing several students to act.

How Does it Move?
by Douglas and Sharman Wurst

▶ **Materials:** paper, pencils, chart paper, marking pen

▶ **Here's How!**

1. Tell students that you will tell them a way that an animal moves. (See example at right.) They will then list on paper as many animals as possible for that category. For example, a list of animals that move with no legs might include snakes, worms, snails, and slugs.

2. After 1 minute, compile student lists on a chart.

3. Continue in this manner with all categories or as time permits.

with wings
butterfly
beetle
dragonfly
bat
birds

on no legs
on two legs
on four legs
on many legs
with wings

Creep, Run, Swim, or Fly

by Martha Cheney

▶ **Materials:** soft foam ball or beanbag

▶ **Here's How!**

1. Begin the game by tossing the ball (or beanbag) to any student.

2. While the ball is in the air, call out a category—creep, run, swim, fly.

3. A student must catch the ball and name an animal that fits in that category.

4. The student then tosses the ball to another classmate and names a category.

5. Play continues in this manner, allowing all students to participate.

What's Missing?
by Martha Cheney

▶ **Materials:** chalkboard, chalk

▶ **Here's How!**

This activity serves as a chance to reinforce students' knowledge about the body structures of familiar animals.

1. Draw a simple picture of an animal on the chalkboard, omitting some essential part of the drawing. (See box below for examples.)

2. Invite a student volunteer to come up and complete the drawing.

3. Discuss the results with the class.

Drawing Examples
spider with only 4 legs
frog with no eyes
bird with no beak
a giraffe with a short neck
skunk with no tail
elephant with no trunk

Earth Layers Chant

by Jo Ellen Moore

▶ **Materials:** none

▶ **Here's How!**

1. Form a small circle of students facing outward. They represent the "inner core" of the earth. Have a second row of students surround the inner core to represent the "outer core."

2. Form a larger circle of students facing outward around the outer core to represent the "mantle."

3. Have seven children form a loose outside circle around the mantle. They represent the "plates of the crust."

4. Finally, assign each group of students a part of the chant.

    a. Students representing the inner and outer cores stamp their feet and chant: *core, core, core.*

    b. Students representing the mantle put their hands out to support the crust, and rock from side to side as they chant: *mantle, mantle, mantle.*

    c. Students representing the plates of the crust move around the circle slowly and chant: *crust, crust, crust.*

5. Once each group knows its part, count to three and have the "earth" begin to move and chant.

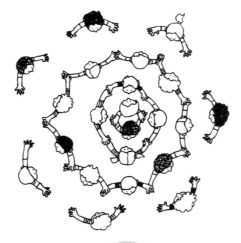

Rotating Solar System
by Laurie Williams

▶ **Materials:** chart paper, marking pen

▶ **Here's How!**

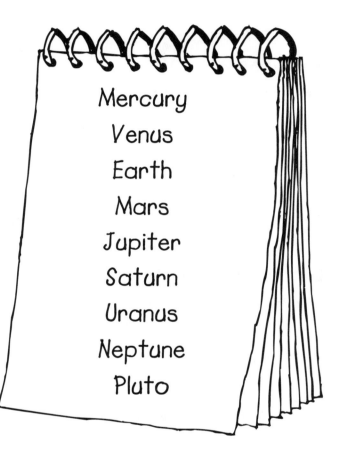

1. List the names of the planets on a chart. Read them aloud with the class in a chanting fashion several times.

2. Have 10 students line up in an open area.

3. The first student represents the Sun and the center of the solar system. The other nine students represent the nine planets in order from the Sun.

4. The student representing the Sun stands still while the students representing the planets rotate around the Sun, staying in their own circle (orbit), so that all planets remain in order. While the planets rotate, have the class chant the names of the planets in order. As each name is said, the student representing that planet is to raise his or her hand.

5. Draw students' attention to the orbital paths of the planets and why a year on Pluto is so much longer than a year on Earth or a year on Mercury.

Here We Grow

by Martha Cheney

▶ **Materials:** none

▶ **Here's How!**

This activity will foster an understanding of the process of growth.

1. Have students stand.

2. Tell students to pretend that they are seeds. Ask students to make themselves as small as possible.

3. Talk to the "seeds" about how comfortable they are, tucked away in the soil. Describe how the warm sun and sweet rain makes them wake up and want to grow.

4. Act out the growth of the plant by gradually beginning to unfold and stretch.

5. Encourage students to imagine the particular type of flower they are growing into as they use their hands and whole bodies to "bloom."

▶ **Variations**

- Act out the growth of a frog from an egg to an adult frog.

- Act out the growth of a butterfly from an egg to an adult.

Habitat Hunt

by Martha Cheney

▶ **Materials:** animal pictures, chart paper, marker

▶ **Here's How!**

1. Show a picture of an animal to the class. This may be a pet, domestic animal, or wild animal. (If possible, post the picture at the top of a piece of chart paper.)

2. Ask students to consider the kind of habitat this animal would need to survive. Remind students to take into account the animal's needs for food and shelter.

3. Beneath the animal's picture, write the students' ideas and suggestions.

▶ **Variation**

Challenge students to identify specific locations in the world where each animal might be found.

river to catch fish

trees for cubs to climb

away from humans

enough space to be away from other bears

place to hibernate

Balancing Act

by Susan Kunze

▶ **Materials:** none

▶ **Here's How!**

1. Have each student stand and balance on one foot while counting to 10.

2. Have everyone take a short rest.

3. Then have students try balancing on one foot again, this time with their eyes closed.

4. Ask questions about this experience such as, "How far can you count to now?" "Was it easier or harder with your eyes closed?" "How can you explain this experience?"

It is more difficult to balance with our eyes closed because our sense of vision tells us our position in relation to the horizon.

Sensory Overload

by Laurie Williams

▶ **Materials:** none

▶ **Here's How!**

1. Choose five students to stand in separate areas of the room.

2. Each of the five students is designated to represent one of the five senses. Throughout the activity:

   - the student representing seeing will point to his or her eyes
   - the student representing touch will hold out his or her hands
   - the student representing hearing/listening will point to his or her ears
   - the student representing taste will stick out his or her tongue
   - the student representing smell will point to his or her nose

3. Ask four to six students to stand.

4. Call out an item that can be sensed and direct students to move to the correct area of the room with the sense represented. Those in their seats decide if the students moved to the correct sense.

5. After the first group has had one or two turns to move to the correct sense, choose a new group of students to participate.

Examples
- Teacher says, "music."
  Students move to "hearing."
- Teacher says, "soft kitten."
  Students move to "touch."
- Teacher says, "sunlight."
  Students move to "seeing" or "touch," if they explain that you can feel the heat of sunlight.
- Teacher says, "chocolate ice cream."
  Students move to "taste" or "touch," if they explain that you can feel the cold of ice cream.
- Teacher says, "bread baking."
  Students move to "smell."

Sound Ideas

by Douglas and Sharman Wurst

▶ **Materials:** wooden rulers

▶ **Here's How!**

1. Pose the question, "Do you think the length of a thing affects the sound that it makes when it vibrates?"

2. Have students place a wooden ruler on the edge of their desks so that most of the ruler hangs over. You might say, "Place the ruler so that the number one is at the edge of the desk."

3. Instruct students to "twang" the end of the ruler and listen carefully to the sound.

4. Instruct students to move the ruler so that the number two is at the edge of the desk and "twang" the ruler. Did the sound change? How?

5. Speculate about what will happen if the ruler is shortened further. Then allow students time to experiment with their rulers.

6. Compare student observations. What conclusions can be drawn? Can students draw any correlation to musical instruments?

As the length of a vibrating object decreases, the rate of vibration increases and the pitch becomes higher.

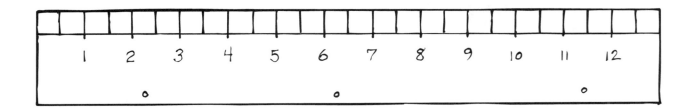

It's in the Bag!

by Doug and Sharman Wurst

▶ **Materials:** one large plastic trash bag, chalkboard, chalk

▶ **Here's How!**

1. Show students a large plastic trash bag. Keep the bag flat and unopened.

2. Gather the open end of the bag so it appears as though you will blow up the bag like a balloon.

3. Ask students to predict how long it will take to fill the bag with air.

4. Write student predictions on the chalkboard.

5. Surprise your students by opening up the bag and scooping air into it. Capture the air by quickly closing and tying off the open end of the bag.

6. Explain that the directions didn't say how to fill the bag; they assumed the bag should be filled by blowing into it. Have a discussion that points out that there may be more than one way to accomplish a task. For example, there may be more than one way to: read an unknown word, find the answer to a math problem, gather information from a science experiment, or solve a problem at recess.

Hang in There
by Douglas and Sharman Wurst

▶ **Materials:** paper

▶ **Here's How!**

1. Give each student a piece of paper.

2. Tell them that they may shape their papers any way they want, so when the paper is dropped it will stay in the air for as long as possible.

3. Allow students just a few minutes to prepare their papers.

4. Have small groups of students, one group at a time, hold their papers at the same height and release them when you say the word *drop.*

5. The student whose paper hits the floor last is the winner.

▶ **Variation**

Have students prepare their papers to see whose paper can hit the floor first.

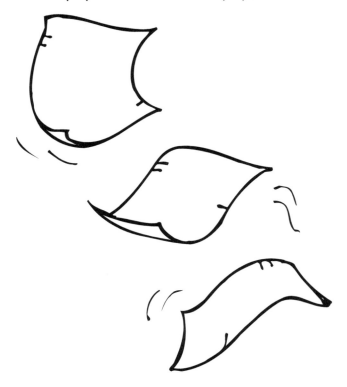

Air Power

by Susan Kunze

▶ **Materials:** 2" x 8" (5 x 20 cm) strips of paper, chalkboard, chalk

▶ **Here's How!**

1. Give each student a strip of paper, telling them they will be asked to lift the strip up using only the power of air.

2. Direct each student to hold one end of the paper strip between the thumb and forefinger. Demonstrate how to raise the held end of the paper strip and place it just below the lower lip.

3. Say, "I am going to blow on this paper. What do you think will happen?" List responses on the chalkboard and tally the number of students choosing each response.

4. Now direct students to blow on their paper strips. Rather than blowing the strip downward, students will notice that the strips rise.

Why It Works

As air moves in a stream, it loses pressure. Pressure becomes lower above the strip than below it. This lowered pressure causes lift, the force that allows airplanes to fly. The faster air moves, the more pressure it loses and the higher the strip flies. This is called Bernoulli's principle and explains how airplanes are able to fly.

"Wood" You Believe It?

by Doug and Sharman Wurst

▶ **Materials:** chalkboard, chalk

▶ **Here's How!**

1. Have the students visually explore the classroom, looking for items made from trees.

2. On the chalkboard, write the names of the items that students find.

3. Discuss the importance of wood in our daily lives.

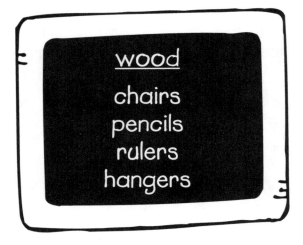

Hop, Pop, and Jump!
by Susan Kunze

▶ **Materials:** a balloon for each student, puffed cereal or small pieces of paper, paper confetti

▶ **Here's How!**

1. Give each student a balloon and place 10 or fewer pieces of puffed cereal or confetti on each desk.

2. Have students blow up their balloons. Twist the ends, but do not tie them off.

3. Rub the balloons back and forth in their hair about 10 times.

4. Then quickly hold the balloon over their cereal or confetti, which will jump onto the balloon and stick to it for a short time.

5. Have students experiment by rubbing their balloons for longer periods of time or by bringing a newly charged balloon near a balloon with puffs or confetti on it.

6. Students hold onto their balloons as they let out the air.

7. Ask helpers to take wastebaskets around to pick up the cereal or confetti.

Why It Works

By rubbing the balloon in your hair, it becomes negatively charged. These negative ions repel the electrons in the puffs or confetti, leaving only the positive ions near the balloon. Since opposites attract, the puffs, confetti, or any other lightweight material can be lifted to the balloon by static electricity.

Can You Do It?

by Susan Kunze

▶**Materials:** straight-back chairs, small objects to pick up

▶**Here's How!**

1. Have students sit back in chairs with their feet together on the floor and arms folded. Ask them to try to stand up without leaning forward or using their arms or hands.

2. Try another impossible task. Have students stand with the right side of their body and right foot directly against a wall and then try to raise their left foot and keep it up.

3. Now have students stand with their back, from head to heels, pressed against the wall. Place a small object (eraser, piece of candy, etc.) approximately 12 inches in front of their feet. Challenge students to pick it up without bending their knees or moving their heels from the wall.

Why It Works

Gravity is the force that pulls everything toward the earth's center. Our center of gravity is in the torso, with our weight evenly balanced around it. Anytime we want to move our muscles, we must overcome the force of gravity pulling on our center. In each of these experiments the position of our center of gravity makes it difficult for our muscles to create enough force to overcome it.

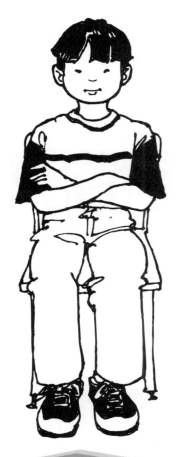

Test Your Strength

by Susan Kunze

▶ **Materials:** several balloons, book

▶ **Here's How!**

1. Blow up a balloon and ask a student to pop it by stepping on it.

2. Then ask students if it's possible that a balloon can be too powerful to pop. Take a vote.

3. Blow up another balloon to approximately the size of the book you will use.

4. Call up a student. Place the book on top of the balloon. Tell the class that the student is going to press down on the book as hard as he or she can. Ask how many students think the balloon will break.

5. Instruct the student to keep the pressure on the balloon evenly with both hands.

6. Still not popped? Call up another student and ask him or her to sit or lie on the balloon.

7. Ask students for ideas as to how the balloon can be so strong. Explain the scientific principle involved.

Why It Works

To pop a balloon, we use direct force in one spot. When pressing on the book, the force is spread out over the whole balloon, so the force does not have the same effect. Hovercraft work in this way as well. By spreading out their weight over a whole cushion of air, they are able to stay above the water.

The Biome Game

by Doug and Sharman Wurst

▶ **Materials:** chalkboard, chalk, paper, pencils

▶ **Here's How!**

arctic

polar bear
moss
lichens
caribou
walrus

1. Divide the class into groups of four or five students.

2. Write a biome on the chalkboard. For example:

   rainforest, ocean, desert, plains, arctic, or conifer forest

3. Give students 60 seconds to write the names of plants and animals that live in that biome.

4. The group with the most correct answers may choose the next biome.

All the Nerve!

by Doug and Sharman Wurst

▶ **Materials:** none

▶ **Here's How!**

This a great activity for your students as they are waiting in line—have them become the nervous system.

1. Students hold hands. The first student in line is a part of the body that receives a stimulus. The last student is the mouth that voices the result of the stimulus.

2. Students sequentially squeeze hands to pass the stimulus.

Examples
- Say, "You are a foot. You have just stepped in cold water." (mouth says, "Brrr!")
- Say, "You are a foot. You have just stepped on a tack." (mouth says, "Ouch!")
- Say, "You are a foot. You have just been tickled with a feather." (mouth says, "Ha, ha, ha!")

No Bones About It!
by Marilyn Evans

▶ **Materials:** none

▶ **Here's How!**

This activity will help students learn the scientific as well as common names for the important bones in their skeletal system.

1. Have students stand beside their desks.

2. Ask them to touch various body parts. Use the common name first, then tell students the scientific name for that part. Ask students to touch the part when using the scientific name. For example:

> "Touch your knee bone.
> The scientific name for your knee bone is patella.
> Touch your patella."

Bones to Use

Common Name	Scientific Name
Shoulder	clavicle
Shoulder blade	scapula
Backbone	spine, vertebral column
Skull	cranium
Breastbone	sternum
Thighbone	femur
Lower-leg bones	tibia, fibula
Upper-arm bone	humerus
Lower-arm bones	radius, ulna
Toes, fingers	phalanges
Tail bone	coccyx
Hipbone	illium

Amazing Memory

by Laurie Williams

▶ **Materials:** various classroom objects, paper, pencils

▶ **Here's How!**

1. Place 20 or 25 objects (see box below) on a flat surface and cover them up.

2. Remove the cover. Invite all students, at the same time, to view the items up close for exactly 1 minute. Cover the items again.

3. When students return to their seats, ask them to write down as many items as they can remember.

4. As a class, list all of the objects students recall. Give a prize to the student who wrote down the greatest number of correct items.

Suggested Objects

pencil, rubber band, stapler, paper clip, thumb tack, ruler, eraser, mouse pad, pen, crayon, marker, glue stick, textbook, hole punch, sticker, candy, envelope, masking tape, protractor, computer disk

Pass It Around

by Eve Timm

▶ **Materials:** a small object (such as a beanbag)

▶ **Here's How!**

1. Teach your students a chant, rhyme, or saying that is easy to learn. Familiar nursery rhymes such as "Mary, Mary," "Little Boy Blue," or "Black Sheep, Black Sheep" are good choices.

2. Have students sit in a circle, hands behind their backs, with one child chosen to sit in the center.

3. While the student in the center covers his or her eyes, the other students pass around the small object behind their backs.

4. The students repeat the chant while the object is passed around. When the chant ends, students stop passing the object.

5. The student in the center opens his or her eyes and attempts to guess who has the object. If guessed correctly, he or she gets another turn. If not, the student holding the object takes the center spot and the process is repeated.

6. Remind the students to keep their hands behind their backs, pretending to have the object, in order to make guessing more difficult.

Motion Sickness

by Laurie Williams

▶ **Materials:** none

▶ **Here's How!**

1. Stand with your students in a circle.

2. Begin by doing a motion such as pinching your nose.

3. The student to your left copies your motion and adds a new one such as hopping on one foot.

4. The next student must remember to pinch his or her nose, hop on one foot, and add another movement.

5. The game gets more complicated as the students continue around the circle.

6. The object is to pay attention and remember all the motions in order and perform them correctly.

7. When a student can't remember a motion or does the wrong one, he or she sits down and the next student continues.

8. The winner is the one left who can do all the motions.

Shoe Salad
by Laurie Williams

▶ **Materials:** students' shoes

▶ **Here's How!**

1. Have all students sit in a circle. Students take off their shoes and put them in a pile in the center of the circle.

2. One student tries to match each pair of shoes to its owner in an allotted amount of time (try 1 minute).

3. When the student is finished matching all the shoes, everyone with the correct pair of shoes in front of them raises their hands.

4. Put the shoes back in the middle of the circle and let another student attempt to match them to their owners.

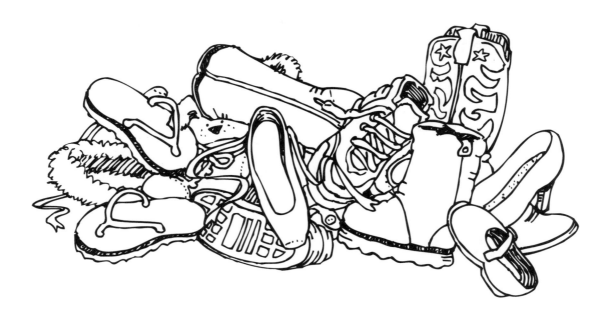

Going on a Field Trip

by Laurie Williams

▶ **Materials:** none

▶ **Here's How!**

1. Have students sit in a circle on the floor.

2. Begin by saying, "I'm going on a field trip and I'm bringing a school bus to take us."

3. The student directly next to you says, for example, "I'm going on a field trip and I'm bringing a school bus and a sack lunch."

4. The object is to remember what each person before has said and recall it in sequence.

▶ **Variation**

For older grades, have students list only things that begin with the same letter of their name.

> For example, a student named **R**eagan would say, "I'm bringing **r**aisins." And a student named **G**lenn would say, "I'm bringing my **g**lasses." Once students understand the pattern, they tell what they would bring.

Other students can help those who are unsure of the rule by saying to a student named Claudia, who doesn't understand the pattern yet, "**C**laudia could bring a **c**amera on the field trip, but she could not bring film."

Eraser Tag

by Laurie Williams

▶ **Materials:** two chalkboard erasers

▶ **Here's How!**

1. Choose one student to be "It."

2. It walks around the room with two chalkboard erasers in hand.

3. It puts an eraser on another student's desk. Both students then place the erasers on their heads. The person who was just chosen tries to tag It. Erasers must remain on top of their heads the whole time.

4. It must circle the room without being tagged and then sit in the second student's desk, keeping the eraser in place. If this is completed successfully, the second student becomes It and repeats steps 2 through 4.

▶ **Variation**

To involve more students in this game, divide students into groups of five or six and have them sit in circles in different areas of the room. Play the game in the same manner with one student in each group being It.

Mannequin

By Laurie Williams

▶ **Materials:** chalkboard, chalk

▶ **Here's How!**

1. Have students sit at their desks or on the floor. Discuss what a mannequin is—not alive, doesn't move, stays in one position, etc.

2. Explain to students that the job in this activity is to be absolutely still, as if one were a mannequin.

3. Choose one student to be "It" by writing his or her initials on the chalkboard.

4. The student who is It comes to the front of the classroom. The "mannequins" are given a chance to assume any pose desired.

5. It says, "Begin," then scans the class, looking for another student who is the quietest and most still.

6. When It decides which student is the most still, he or she writes the initials of that student on the board.

7. The new It comes to the front of the classroom and the game begins again.

That's Me!

by Eve Timm

▶ **Materials:** none

▶ **Here's How!**

1. The object of this game is for the students to try to guess who is being talked about.

2. Begin to give very general clues, getting more specific as you go. "This is a first-grader. This is a boy. This is a boy who has six letters in his first name. This boy has two sisters," etc.

3. Continue until one student identifies himself or herself as the featured student.

Invisible Recess

by Jennifer Norris

▶ **Materials:** chalkboard, chalk

▶ **Here's How!**

1. Begin by listing on the chalkboard the equipment found on the playground. If the equipment at your school is limited, list items students have seen on other playgrounds. For example:

   monkey bars, jungle gym, swings, teeter-totter, slide, merry-go-round

2. Ask students to imagine that they can play on any piece of playground equipment.

3. Call on a student to pantomime something he or she would do on the equipment.

4. The other students try to guess what activity is being portrayed.

5. The student who guesses correctly gets to do the next pantomime.

Telephone Lines

by Jennifer Norris

▶ **Materials:** none

▶ **Here's How!**

1. Have students sit in a circle on the floor. (If you have a large class, form several circles to allow more frequent participation.)

2. Whisper a sentence into one student's ear such as, "Whales migrate in the spring."

3. Students whisper the phrase to their neighbors, in turn, until the last person in the circle repeats the phrase aloud.

4. After having a good laugh at how the phrase became turned around, start a new phrase in the opposite direction.

▶ **Variation**

Allow a student to start the sentence. Have the student tell you before beginning.

Possible Phrases
• Why did Sam save so many stamps?
• Mary moved to Florida on the first of March.
• I saw a seagull flying at the seashore.

A What?

by Jennifer Norris

▶ **Materials:** any small classroom object

▶ **Here's How!**

1. Form a circle, either sitting or standing, with your students.

2. Hand the object to the first student to your right and say, "This is an elephant."

3. The student responds, "A what?"

4. You answer, "An elephant."

5. The process repeats itself around the circle.

> Student 2 to Student 3: "This is an elephant."
> Student 3 to Student 2: "A what?"
> Student 2 to Student 1: "A what?"
> Student 1 to Teacher: "A what?"
> Teacher to Student 1: "An elephant."
> Student 1 to Student 2: "An elephant."
> Student 2 to Student 3: "An elephant."
> Student 3 to Student 4: "This is an elephant."

▶ **Variation**

Start a second object (a rhinoceros) simultaneously in the opposite direction.

Pass the Button

by Doug and Sharman Wurst

▶ **Materials:** a button or any small object

▶ **Here's How!**

1. Have students sit on the floor in two rows, facing each other.

2. Choose one of the rows to pass the button first. Everyone in that row holds their hands in front of their body with fists closed.

3. Let everyone see you place the button in one person's hand.

4. The object is to pass the button without the other team knowing where the button is. All students may pretend to pass the button to the next person in line, even if they do not actually have it. Students' hands must remain visible at all times.

5. The button is passed for 30 seconds.

6. When time is up, all students put their hands in their laps, fists closed.

7. Students in the opposite row point to the person they think has the button.

8. The person who has the most students pointing at him or her shows whether he or she has the button.

9. If the person has the button, the team guessing gets one point. If that person does not have the button, the team with the button gets one point.

10. Now the other team gets to take a turn passing the button.

Hide and Sing

by Doug and Sharman Wurst

▶ **Materials:** a small object

▶ **Here's How!**

1. Select a person to be "It."

2. It waits out of the room while another student hides a secret object.

3. The object is hidden in plain sight.

4. It is brought back into the room.

5. The class sings a favorite song, gradually singing louder when It walks toward the object and softer when It walks away from the object.

6. It has 1 minute to find the object.

7. Continue in this manner, allowing different students to be It.

Yardstick Limbo

by Doug and Sharman Wurst

▶ **Materials:** a yardstick, an exercise mat, a recording of lively music

▶ **Here's How!**

1. Have two students hold a yardstick horizontally between them at shoulder height.

2. The other students form a line and dance to the music as they "limbo" under the yardstick. (Students may go under the stick in any manner they choose.)

3. Any student who knocks the stick down is out.

4. Once everyone has been given the chance to limbo under the stick the first time, the stick is lowered.

5. The process continues until there is only one person left.

Eraser Relay

by Susan Kunze

▶ **Materials:** several chalkboard erasers, masking tape (optional)

▶ **Here's How!**

1. Divide students into any number of equal-sized teams. Have teams sit in rows. They may sit in desks, chairs, or on the floor. If they are on the floor, mark the beginning of each row with a strip of masking tape.

2. The first student in each row is given an eraser and then passes it overhead to the student behind him or her. Students continue passing the eraser in this manner.

3. When the eraser is received by the last student in the row, he or she rushes up to the starting point. Everyone in the row moves back one place, and passing the eraser begins again.

4. The first team with all of its players back in their original positions wins.

Holding the Bag
by Susan Kunze

▶ **Materials:** beanbag, bell or whistle

▶ **Here's How!**

1. Have students sit in a circle. Instruct them to pass the beanbag quickly around the circle.

2. Have one student sit with his or her back to the circle. This student periodically rings a bell or blows a whistle and turns around to face the circle.

3. A student who is caught holding the bag at the signal must raise one hand, but may continue playing with the other hand.

4. Students caught a second time place both hands behind their backs. They continue playing by passing the bag with hands still behind their backs, even if caught again.

5. The game continues until only one player is left passing the bag with both hands in front of him or her.

Statue

by Douglas and Sharman Wurst

▶ **Materials:** none

▶ **Here's How!**

1. Sing a simple song or clap a repeating rhythm for your students.

2. Have students walk around the room to the song or rhythm.

3. Tell students that when the song stops, they must freeze like a statue in a specific manner. For example:

   on one foot
   with hands above shoulders
   with hands on head

4. Any student who is caught moving or is not posed appropriately must sit down.

5. The game continues until there is only one student standing.

Find a Seat

by Susan Kunze

▶ **Materials:** none

▶ **Here's How!**

1. Have students sit in their seats. A "runner" stands at the front of the room. A "chaser" stands in the back of the room.

2. Make sure students understand that only walking is allowed. If either the runner or the chaser runs, they will lose their turn.

3. On a signal, the chaser chases the runner.

4. The runner tries to escape being tagged by sitting in a seat beside someone else. That student becomes the new chaser, and the previous chaser now becomes the runner.

5. If the chaser does tag the runner before he or she reaches a chair, each one chooses another student to take his or her place.

▶ **Variation**

For more of a challenge, require the runner and chaser to only run up and down rows, rather than between desks.

Honk! Honk!

by Susan Kunze

▶ **Materials:** masking tape (optional)

▶ **Here's How!**

1. Divide students into equal teams. Students sit in rows. They may sit in desks, chairs, or on the floor. If they are on the floor, mark the beginning of each row with a strip of masking tape. Assign the name of an automobile to each team.

2. When you give the signal, "Honk! Honk!" the game begins. The first player on each team puts his or her car into gear and walks quickly all the way around the row. (Encourage the use of other car sound effects.)

3. After completing the course, the player sits down and turns to the person behind him or her and says, "Honk! Honk!" This is the signal for the next player to warm up his or her engine and go.

4. When all players on a team have completed the course, the entire team stands and says, "Honk! Honk!" The first team to honk wins the game!

Silent Ball

by Susan Kunze

▶ **Materials:** a beach ball

▶ **Here's How!**

1. Have students sit on their desks with their legs hanging down. Students may shift in any direction, but their feet and lower legs must remain off the desktop.

2. One student quickly throws the beach ball to any other student. If the student fails to catch it, he or she is out and sits in his or her chair. If the throw is short, the thrower is out. In addition, anyone making noise during the game is out. It's tough to remain silent, because excitement runs high!

3. Students continue to throw the ball until only one player is left. This player is declared the winner and a new game begins.

It is sometimes difficult for students to agree whether a throw is short, etc. Instead of stalling the game, choose a "judge" to watch the game and point to any fouling player. The judge's rulings are final and not subject to debate. The winner of the game becomes the judge of the next game.